The Girl's Guide to

Friendship!

An imprint of Hendrickson Publishers Marketing, LLC.
Peabody, Massachusetts
www.HendricksonRose.com

Check out all of the books in The Girl's Guide series:

The Girl's Guide to

Friendship!

Kathy Widenhouse

To Britta, my own precious God's girl!

THE GIRL'S GUIDE TO FRIENDSHIP
©2014 by Kathy Widenhouse

RoseKidz®
An imprint of Hendrickson Publishers Marketing, LLC.
P. O. Box 3473, Peabody
Massachusetts 01961-3473
www.HendricksonRose.com

Register your book at www. HendricksonRose.com/register and receive a free Bible Reference download.

Cover and Interior Illustrator: Anita DuFalla

ISBN 10: 1-58411-043-0
ISBN 13: 978-1-58411-043-9
RoseKidz® reorder# L48212
JUVENILE NONFICTION / Religion / Christianity / Christian Life

Printed in South Korea   18   04.2017.APC

Table of Contents

Hey, Girlfriend!

Never will I leave you; never will I forsake you.
~Hebrews 13:5

I'm excited you are reading this book! It means that you want to have fantastic friends...and be one, too.

Until recently, your parents have helped pave the way in your world (that's their job!), especially in one big area: friendship. They encouraged you when you picked friends who they thought were a good fit for you...girls at school, scouts, church, clubs, sports teams or in the neighborhood. Your parents helped with much of the legwork: they suggested activities for you and your friends, and made a lot of the arrangements. Along the way, your parents tried to teach you some Friendship Basics: they pointed out your friends' nice qualities, broke up your arguments, wiped your tears when you got hurt–and complimented you when you were being a good friend.

Mom and Dad have done a good job, but you're growing up. You've formed your own ideas about friendship. So now...

It's your turn!

You are at a new stage in your life: you are becoming more independent. (Your parents know it, too, but be patient with them...it might take them a little longer to catch up with you!) You might be changing schools, becoming more involved in extra activities, making some of your own decisions and discovering your strengths for yourself.

During this time of changes, you will now be taking the lead in choosing your friends and learning how to be a good friend to them. Friends your own age (called your "peers") are important to you right now because:

They relate to you–both of you are growing up at the same time.

They are learning right alongside you–you are *not* alone.

They make you feel good about you–they choose to be your friend.

It is exciting, scary and complicated all at the same time!

It's **exciting** because you are making your own choices.

It's **SCARY** because you've got more responsibility.

It's **COMPLICATED** because you get a lot of advice from a lot of different people.

This book is a guide! Learning about friendship is fun–and **confusing!**

But **YOU** –*God's girl*–have a distinct advantage. You are friends with Jesus, your A.B.F.F. (*Absolute Best Friend Forever*). And since He's already been through it all–every happy and mixed-up feeling you are having or will have about friendship–He can help you through it. He can even help you be better friends with Him, because sometimes that's confusing, too.

What can get hard is putting it all together. You are learning to navigate it as God's girl.

That's where The Christian Girl's Guide to Friendship comes in!

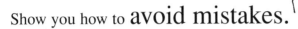

This book will...

Point to some **new ideas**.

Help you **sort things out**.

Give you **encouragement** when you're on the right track.

Show you how to **avoid mistakes.**

Teach you to be **a great friend,** and have terrific friends–now and for the rest of your life!

You can use this book in many ways

Read it on your own, just to find out about making friends.

Use it **during your devotions** and ask God to teach you through it.

Keep it handy, and refer to it when you have a question or problem with your friends.

Share it with your friends, and talk about what you learned.

Show it to **your church's teachers**, leaders and youth workers.

They might even want to use it as a resource at some of your group meetings!

Friends for life!

Learning about friendship doesn't happen all at once. It's a process. By getting a good start so soon, you have the opportunity to have fantastic friends and be one, too… throughout your entire life!

One last thing...remember that your A.B.F.F. is with you every step of the way.

God Puts It This Way

Never will I leave you; never will I forsake you.

~ Hebrews 13:5

Your F.I.J.*,

Kathy Widenhouse

*see chapter 11!

Chapter One

Friends & Friendship

"Two are better than one."

~Ecclesiastes 4:9

✻ Friendship Is a Gift ✻

Friendship is a gift you give to others, and others give to you.

It is special because…

There is **no one** exactly like **you.** Your friendship is one-of-a-kind!

No one can force you to be a friend. You choose to give the gift of friendship.

Like any gift, friendship can…

✻ Take time to find. (You know how long it takes to find that perfect gift!)

✻ Cost something, such as time, energy or patience.

✻ Be unique for each person you know.

✻ Break.

✻ Be exchanged, returned or last forever.

God Puts It This Way

Freely you have received, freely give.

~Matthew 10:8

Write About It

Write God a thank You note for the gift of friendship, and list all your friends (your gifts!) by name.

_____

_____

_____

QUIZ! What's Fair to Expect from a Friend?

Sometimes being a friend is confusing. We want friends who are faithful and fun. Yet we may expect more from a friend than what is really fair. What's true...and what's not? Choose what you think is true or not.

1 A friend isn't really a friend unless she likes everything about you.

> True   Not true

2 Friends must tell each other every personal secret or they are not really friends.

> True   Not true

3 If your friend doesn't ask you to be her partner in the science fair project, she's not really your friend.

> True   Not true

4 You meet a new girl at softball practice. You think you'd like to get to know her better, but then you find out she doesn't go to church. Too bad...now you can't be friends with her.

> True   Not true

5 Aileen made a mistake that hurt you: she ignored you when you told her your worries about your new braces. Later, she apologized. Even so, you can't be friends anymore.

> True   Not true

✓ Check your answers!

1. **Not true!** Friends don't expect their friends to be perfect. No one is perfect!

2. **Not true!** Friends share secrets with each other because they want to, not because they have to.

3. **Not true!** Friends can have more than one friend. And they don't take any of their friends for granted.

4. **Not true!** Jesus made lots of friends with people who didn't go to church. By being friends with them, He helped them grow closer to God.

5. **Not true!** Everyone makes mistakes. Friends forgive friends, and they ask for forgiveness when they mess up, too.

 ## God Puts It This Way
For God is not a God of disorder but of peace.
~1 Corinthians 14:33

 ## Talk to God

Dear God, thank You for (name a friend). I confess that I am confused about my friendship with her because (why you are confused). Show me Your way of looking at this friendship. Help me find one way today to appreciate this friend and thank her for her friendship. In Jesus' name, Amen.

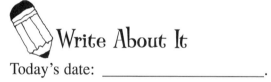 ## Write About It

Today's date: _____.

Think about the friendship for which you just prayed. List below all of the qualities in your friend that are really terrific–and that perhaps you take for granted. Try to show your friend appreciation each day that you see her, then in a few weeks, re-read this entry and see if your expectations of your friend have changed!

_____

_____

_____

♪ A Note to Myself

Re-read this entry on _____.

The Friendship Top 10

All girls agree: a real friend has certain characteristics. When you see these qualities in another person, take note–she has the makings to become your true and treasured friend. Here's your Friendship Top 10:

 1 A friend likes you for you.

 ### God Puts It This Way
A friend loves at all times.
~Proverbs 17:17

DO YOU WANT TO GO TO THE BASKETBALL GAME?

SURE, AND MAYBE WE CAN GET ICE CREAM AFTER.

 2 A friend makes doing things as two more fun than one.

God Puts It This Way
Two are better than one.
~Ecclesiastes 4:9

 3 A friend is someone you can trust.

God Puts It This Way
A trustworthy man keeps a secret.
~Proverbs 11:13

 4 A friend sticks with you in the good and bad times.

God Puts It This Way
Rejoice with those who rejoice; mourn with those who mourn.
~Romans 12:15

 5 A friend appreciates your special qualities.

God Puts It This Way
Whatever is admirable–if anything is excellent or praiseworthy – think about such things.
~Philippians 4:8

6 A friend helps you and shares her stuff with you.

 ## God Puts It This Way

If one falls down, his friend can help him up.

~Ecclesiastes 4:10

7 A friend is honest with you, even when it is hard to be.

 ## God Puts It This Way

Wounds from a friend can be trusted.

~Proverbs 27:6

8 A friend listens.

 ## God Puts It This Way

Be quick to listen, slow to speak.

~James 1:19

9 A friend forgives you and asks for your forgiveness.

 ## God Puts It This Way

Be kind and compassionate to one another, forgiving each other.

~Ephesians 4:32

10 A friend is fun to be with!

 ## God Puts It This Way

Rejoice in the Lord always. I will say it again: Rejoice!

~Philippians 4:4

Talk to God

Dear God, thank You for the good friends You have given me (name some friends). I appreciate this special quality in my friend (name your favorite quality and a friend who exhibits it). Help me seek out friends that have these strengths. Thanks for the spotlight on Your Word! In Jesus' name, Amen.

Write About It

Was there an item on the Top 10 list that was new to you? Write it below. Then think of a friend who shows that quality and describe what she does to exhibit it.

_____

_____

_____

FAQs: Friendship Experts

Does it seem like everyone around you is an "expert" on friendship? What's a girl to think? Read on!

Who Tells Whom

Q: There's a group of girls in school who tell me with whom I can be friends. It bugs me because they want to boss me around, but it scares me because they are so powerful.

A: Girls who are less assertive let bossier girls bully them…and before long, the bossy girls have a reputation for being "powerful." Eventually, most girls learn that friendship isn't an item on a menu that they order for someone else. Until others figure this out, make sure you order your own meal! In other words, you should decide who your friends are–with one condition: your parents, as usual, have final approval rights.

Parents

Q: My parents don't get it. They can see that I'm growing up. But they think they can still choose my friends for me because they "know me so well." Help!

A: You are absolutely right: your parents can see that you are growing up. They were your age once, too (a long, looooong time ago), and they want you to avoid some of the pain and mistakes they experienced. That's a big reason why they always want to tell you what to do about your friends.

☞ Try this:

Think of your parents as Experienced Friend-Making Resources, not the enemy. Ask them…

✳ How did you go about making friends when you were my age, and how do you do it now?

✳ What qualities about my friends do you like?

✳ Would you be willing to let me try a few things my way? (specify one or two things to get started)

Friendship Experts

Q: Some girls are experts on friendship. They know who is friends with whom, who is mad at whom and what should be done about it. I want to be an expert, too.

A: Whew, it takes a lot of effort to gather and dole out all that information! Those girls must spend a lot of time whispering, talking and interfering in order to keep up with it all. Most people call this "gossip." Perhaps you are confusing friendship with gossip–in which case, these girls are not experts on friendship at all!

The Group

Q: Sometimes I feel kind of foolish because I choose my own friends rather than following The Group. Other girls seem to completely trust The Group. Am I weird?

A: Don't be so sure that other girls are completely, 100 percent happy following the joint decisions of The Group–especially when The Group does something unkind or unfair. The truth is this: girls in The Group aren't really friendship experts. They are people who are learning and growing…just like you.

Help!

Q: I want to make friends and do it well, but it sounds like I am going to have to go at it all alone. Is there an expert anywhere (not a geek) who can help me?

A: Consult with the One who invented friendship in the first place. Not only is He the expert on friendship, but He is also totally cool. Plus, He really wants your friendships to work for you. He has a personalized friendship plan for you–and will coach you through it. That's why we're calling Him **The Friendship Coach.** Who is this Coach? He's God, of course!

God Puts It This Way

But the plans of the Lord stand firm forever, the purposes of his heart through all generations.

~ Psalm 33:11

Talk to God

Dear God, thank You that you are the friendship expert. Lots of people want to give me friendship advice (name the advice you have received recently, and who gave it to you). I am having a hard time figuring out what is good advice and bad advice, particularly in this situation (name some advice that is confusing). Help me to hear Your advice and follow it. In Jesus' name, Amen.

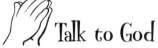

Spotlight On...

The Friendship Coach

As you learn about making friends and being one, have you ever felt…

(Check all that apply)

❏ Different from everyone else?

❏ Silly or stupid?

❏ Confused and scared?

❏ Frustrated?

❏ All alone?

If you checked any boxes above, here is a surprise: You have someone very special on your side…God, **The Friendship Coach!**

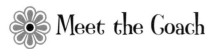 Meet the Coach

Title and Position: Lord God Almighty

Also known as: Father, Jesus, The Holy Spirit, The Rock, The Most High, Teacher, The King of Kings, The Counselor and dozens more.

Qualifications: He invented friendship, so He totally understands how friendship works. He designed the plays and the rules, and He knows the athletes better than anyone.

Experience: Unsurpassed and ongoing. God has coached zillions of girls who have become the world's most outstanding friends. Moreover, He Himself is known as the A.B.F.F. (see chapter 12).

Greatest achievements: Too numerous to list. However, His best, most important achievement was Jesus Christ, His Son, who died on a cross for our sins.

Defeats or setbacks: None. Zero. Nada. Now and forever.

Noteworthy personal attributes: Omnipotent (all-powerful), omniscient (knows everything about everyone), omnipresent (always available).

Publications: The Bible (the all-time best seller!)

The Friendship Coach's coaching techniques: Athletes meet one-on-one with the Coach in prayer for personal instructions. They study and memorize plays from the Bible. The older athletes help the younger ones. These athletes are also automatic members of the Coach's recruiting squad.

Special friendship coaching feature for girls: The Friendship Coach provides a personalized, individual game plan for each member of His team.

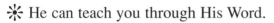

What does this mean for you?

Since you are on God's team, God has a special, individualized game plan for you. Here is how God can coach you through His game plan as you read this book:

❋ He can teach you through His Word.

❋ He can listen to you and talk to you in prayer.

Let's go!

God Puts It This Way

If God is for us, who can be against us?

~ Romans 8:31

Talk to God

Dear God, thanks for inventing friendship! I am glad that I am on Your team, and that You want me to win at **The Friendship Game.** Lately I have felt badly about making friends and being one when (name a situation that made you feel bad). Please take this confusing situation (name it again) and show me what play is next (pause and listen to what God says to your heart, and repeat it back to Him). Help me to follow through with what You are telling me. Remind me during the day today to count on You to be my **Friendship Coach**! In Jesus' name, Amen.

Write About It

Record some new things you learned today about God, your **Friendship Coach**:

_____

_____

_____

The Coach's Take on Friendship

God's Top 10

Q: My friend doesn't go to church, but she read **The Friendship Top 10**. She was shocked! She couldn't believe that God describes a friend the same way we do. How can that be?

A: She's not the only one! It comes as a surprise to many girls that the **Friendship Top 10** is also **The Friendship Coach's** Top 10. God created all people. He programmed us to appreciate qualities in others that build us up and encourage us. That's why His ideas about friendship work for everybody.

The Invisible Coach

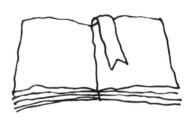

Q: I get discouraged that I can't actually see God. Sometimes I think He is the "Invisible Coach."

A: Many people think that God is not able to coach us about friendship (or anything else) because we can't physically see or touch Him. Yet they forget that we learn from history without physically seeing or touching Marco Polo or George Washington. The truth is this: God does show Himself–but in different ways than we're used to. One way God shows Himself and teaches us about friendship (and everything else!) is through His Word, The Bible.

 ## God Puts It This Way

[God's] word is truth.
~John 17:17

Does God Want Me to Have Friends?

Q: Is it really true…God actually wants me to have friends? I find it hard to believe.

A: God absolutely wants you to have friends. Don't forget: Friendship was God's idea! Here's why:

✳ He wants you to have companionship and not be lonely.

God Puts It This Way
Two are better than one.

~ Ecclesiastes 4:9

✳ He wants you to have friends so you can learn from each other.

God Puts It This Way
As iron sharpens iron, so one man sharpens another.

~ Proverbs 27:17

✳ He wants you to have friends so you can support and encourage each other.

God Puts It This Way
Dear friends, let us love one another, for love comes from God.

~ 1 John 4:7

Talk to God

Dear God, wow, You want me to have friends. Thanks for (name your friends). My friends have helped me to not be lonely. Show us how to learn from, support and encourage each other. In Jesus' name, Amen.

Write About It

Think of a good friend. Write about a time…

✳ Your friend helped you not be lonely, or

✳ You learned something from your friend, or

✳ Your friend supported and encouraged you, or

✳ You supported and encouraged your friend.

_____

_____

_____

Make It! • Note to Myself Memo Pad

When you see ♪ in *The Christian Girl's Guide to Friendship*, you know it's time to write a note to yourself. Make the **A Note to Myself Memo Pad** to help you keep track of these special pages. Use the removable self-stick notes to mark the spots where you leave a note to yourself.

 ## What you need

✳ patterns from page 29

✳ craft foam

✳ self-stick note pad, 1½" x 2"

✳ ball key chain

✳ Velcro®, ½" x ½"

✳ tracing paper

✳ poster board or cardboard

✳ pencil

✳ scissors

✳ hole punch

✳ craft glue

✳ hot glue gun

What to Do

1. With tracing paper and pencil, trace the memo pad cover and music note patterns. Cut out the patterns. Use the patterns and a pencil to outline templates on poster board or cardboard. Cut out the templates.

2. Use the poster board templates as patterns to outline and cut out a memo pad cover and music note decorations from craft foam.

3. Mark the center of the top edge of the craft foam memo pad cover as shown on the pattern. Use the hole punch to punch a hole for the ball key chain.

4. With craft glue, attach a removable self-stick note pad to the craft foam memo pad's inside back cover.

5. With craft glue, attach the music note decorations to the memo pad front cover.

6. Separate the Velcro® into two pieces. Ask an adult to help you with the hot glue gun. Use the hot glue gun to attach one piece of Velcro® to the memo pad's inside front flap. Hot glue the other piece of Velcro® to the back of the memo pad.

7. Allow your memo pad to dry completely. Then, thread the ball key chain through the hole and clip the ball into its casing to secure.

8. Write yourself a note with your new **A Note to Myself Memo Pad!**

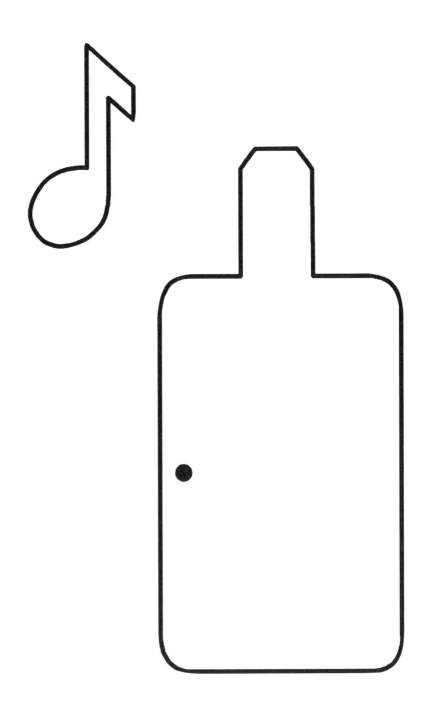

Chapter Two

The Secret to Friendship

"A man reaps what he sows."

~Galatians 6:7

Spotlight On...

The Girl With All the Friends

You know who we're talking about here: everybody likes her, everybody wants to be friends with her. She's...

The Girl With All the Friends!

What's Her Secret?

The Girl With All the Friends knows that her Secret is not really a secret at all. In fact, she learned the Secret from **The Friendship Coach**–and she can pass it along to you. The Secret is this:

> There is one absolutely surefire, positively, totally 100 percent guaranteed thing you need to do in order to have friends.

What is it? Turn the page and check the box for what you think it is...then read on to find out the Secret.

The secret to friendship is to...

☐ 1. Be gorgeous. Then everyone will adore you.

☐ 2. Have all the latest clothes. Everyone will hang around you for free fashion tips.

☐ 3. Excel in sports, art, music, theatre or another special skill. That way, when you become famous everyone who has ever known you will want to be your friend.

☐ 4. Be smarter than anyone else. Everyone will want to be around you just to absorb knowledge.

☐ 5. Become the expert on determining who is cool and who isn't cool. Then everyone will want to be your friend to get the Seal of Cool Approval.

☐ 6. Hang around with the popular group. Their popularity will rub off on you.

☐ 7. Be a good friend. Everyone wants one, and no one can ever have too many.

Read on to find out the Secret...

The Secret to Beauty

If you checked...

1. Be gorgeous.
>   **or**

2. Have all the latest clothes.

Then consider this: beauty is only skin deep. Perhaps you think people will like you (or not like you) just because of your looks. But some of the world's most beautiful or well-dressed people are also the loneliest!

God Puts It This Way

Charm is deceptive, and beauty is fleeting; but a woman who fears the Lord is to be praised.

~ Proverbs 31:30

What God Means Is

Your "inside" beauty is more precious and attractive than your "outside" beauty.

 ## Try This

Find ways to show kindness, caring and thoughtfulness to other people. You will please God as you become more beautiful on the inside. You will also have more friends than you can count!

 ## Talk to God

Dear God, I want to be pretty. Thank you that you gave me (name one of your own physical attributes that you like). But I know that you want me to be beautiful on the inside. Help me to be (name one way you want to grow in your inner beauty). Give me a chance to show this quality to a friend today. In Jesus' name, Amen.

 ## Write About It

What kinds of inner qualities do you think are beautiful?

_____

_____

Read on to find out more Secrets...

The Secret to Success

If you checked...

3. Excel in sports, art, music, theatre or another special skill.
    or
4. Be smarter than anyone else.

Then consider this: excel for the right reasons! Do you work hard on your special gifts in order to improve yourself, or are you working hard so that other people will admire you?

Warning! Warning!

You may think you need to earn friends by getting them to think of you as a star. But some of the world's most famous entertainers, smartest scientists and successful athletes have thousands of admirers–but few real friends.

People won't necessarily become your friends because of your achievements. Instead, they will become your friends because of how you treat them: with respect, appreciation and admiration for what they do.

God Puts It This Way

Whatever you do, work at it with all your heart, as working for the Lord, not for men.

~ Colossians 3:23

What God Means Is

Do everything to please God, not to get people to like you.

Try This

Keep working hard at what you do. At the same time:

❋ notice,

❋ appreciate, and

❋ compliment others on the special gifts you see in them.

That way…

❋ you will please God.

❋ you will respect yourself for using your gifts for the right reasons.

✷ you will have more appreciated and appreciative friends than you can count!

Talk to God

Dear God, thank You for giving me (name one of your own unique traits or abilities). I know that You also want me to appreciate others' special gifts. Help me see strengths in others. Give me the chance to notice and compliment a friend today. In Jesus' name, Amen.

Write About It

What kinds of things do you notice in others that deserve a compliment from you?

_____

_____

Read on to find out more Secrets...

The Secret to Acceptance

If you checked...

5. Become the expert on determining who is cool and who isn't cool.

   or

6. Hang around with the popular group.

Then consider this: think for yourself. It's easy to believe that you can make a lot of friends using the "popular by association" method. Here's how it works:

✷ You study who is popular and cool.

✷ You make changes to yourself in order to be liked by those kids– whether or not you are comfortable with those changes.

✳ You become one of them. Presto: you have a lot of friends!

Uh, oh. A little problem here. What happens when the changes that you make aren't really you? Sooner or later, you realize that people don't necessarily like you for you.

Here's a surprise: everyone wants to be accepted for who they really are. (Even kids who are popular and cool!)

God Puts It This Way

Be strong in the Lord and in his mighty power.

~ Ephesians 6:10

What God Means Is

Remember who you are…God's girl! Be true to yourself and to God. He will help you, especially when you ask Him.

Try This

When you are thinking about making some changes…

✳ Ask yourself, "Is this really who or what I want to be?"

✳ Ask God, "Is this what You want?"

That way…

✳ You will be true to yourself and true to God.

✳ You will make people around you feel comfortable and accepted.

✳ You will discover a surprise…you will have many friends who like the real you.

Talk to God

Dear God, thank You for making me the way I am. Sometimes it is easy to know what is me and what is not me, like when (name one good choice you have made). But sometimes I am not sure, like when (name a confusing situation). What do You think about that situation? Help me be true to me and to You today. In Jesus' name, Amen.

Write About It

Jot down some words that describe the real YOU.

_____

_____

_____

Read on to find out more Secrets…

The Real Secret!

If you checked…

7. Be a good friend.

Then consider this: You know the secret to friendship!

> **Be a good friend. Everyone wants one and no one can ever have too many!**

Don't you feel great when someone reaches out to you? You love it when she shows kindness, respect, thoughtfulness and caring toward you. It's great fun when someone likes you and wants to do things with you. That's called being a friend!

"The only way to have a friend is to be one." Most people give the credit for that idea to the American writer Ralph Waldo Emerson. But guess who said it first?

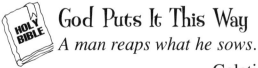

God Puts It This Way

A man reaps what he sows.

~ Galatians 6:7

What God Means Is

When you act like a good friend to someone else, you are sowing seeds of friendship.

 ## Try This

Be a friend!

That way…

✳ You'll please God.

✳ You'll feel happy and confident, knowing you are doing things right.

✳ You'll always have more friends than you can count.

 ## Talk to God

Dear God, thank You for the friends You have given me (name them). I know that You want me to be a friend to others. Bring someone into my life who needs a friend. Help me to notice her, and remind me to sow some friendship seeds with her today. In Jesus' name, Amen.

 ## Write About It

The Secret to Friendship is simple! Why don't more girls know it?

_____

_____

_____

● Make It! ● Stick 2 U Stickers

Stickers are like good friends. They are fun–and they stick to you, no matter what! Make your own **Stick 2 U Stickers** to use on papers, letters and notebooks. Be sure to make plenty of extras to give away to your friends!

 ## What You Need

- ✳ colorful paper, gift wrap or used greeting cards
- ✳ markers
- ✳ white vinegar
- ✳ four 1-oz. packets unflavored gelatin
- ✳ mint extract
- ✳ mixing spoon
- ✳ measuring spoons
- ✳ saucepan
- ✳ paintbrush
- ✳ scissors

What to Do

1. With markers, draw sticker designs on colorful paper. Or, choose designs on gift wrap or used greeting cards to be your stickers.

2. Measure 8 tablespoons of white vinegar into the saucepan. Ask an adult to help you use the stove. Bring the vinegar to a boil. Add four 1-oz. packets of unflavored gelatin. Reduce heat to low. Stir mixture continuously until the gelatin is dissolved. To complete the sticker "glue," measure 1 tablespoon of mint extract and add it to the vinegar-gelatin mixture, stirring thoroughly. Remove from heat.

3. With a paintbrush, apply the sticker glue evenly to the back of the pre-colored sticker drawings or gift wrap. Allow the glue to dry.

4. Cut out your stickers. Moisten the backs of your new **Stick 2 U Stickers** and decorate your papers, letters and notebooks. They will stick just like a loyal friend sticks to her friends!

Hint: Store the remaining sticker glue in an airtight container. The glue will solidify when it cools. You can re-use leftovers by re-warming the airtight container in a bowl of hot water so the glue melts.

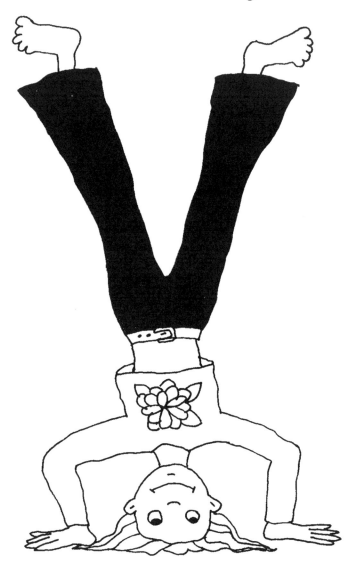

Chapter Three

Measuring You

"You are precious and honored in my sight, and...I love you."
~Isaiah 43:4

✳ The Comparison Game ✳

It's difficult just to be you when you're trying so hard to fit in. You want to be accepted by others–and accept yourself. What do you use to measure yourself?

QUIZ! How Do I Measure Up?

For each question, choose the answer that best describes you. Add up your points and check your total at the end!

1 It's picture day at school. You…

A. Wash, dry and comb your hair, wear your favorite outfit, put on a necklace, and say to yourself, "Might as well look the best I can!"

B. Put on a pink sweater. Look in the mirror. Remember that Mandy, the prettiest girl in your class, never wears pink. Change to a red top.

C. Worry about and plan for picture day for weeks. When you get to school, you are in a panic. Everyone looks better than you, you think.

2 It's time to turn in the fundraiser orders. You…

A. Hand them in.

B. Strain to listen to others when they talk about what they sold and to whom.

C. Ask everyone you see, "How much did you sell?"

3 You are invited to two birthday parties in one week. You…

A. Check the calendar to make sure you can attend, and then find a time to shop for gifts.

B. Ask around to see who is attending which party, or both.

C. Feel completely awful when you learn that Zoe was invited to three parties the same week. Why weren't you?

4. Mrs. Hance passes back the math tests. You…

A. Look at the 84% on your paper and think, *I earned that!*

B. Look at the 84% on your paper and think, *I wonder what everyone else got?*

C. Look at the 84% on your paper and think, *I did worse than everyone else!*

5. You're at the gymnastics meet. You…

A. Are thrilled with your third-place ribbon on the uneven bars. It more than makes up for your fall off the balance beam.

B. Finger your third-place ribbon happily, and look around to see how many other girls on your team received–or didn't receive–prizes.

C. Try to conceal your disappointment as you look down at your third-place ribbon. Samantha has four ribbons and Andrea has two.

6. Debbie, your youth group leader, assigns parts for the Easter pageant. You…

A. See that you have 16 lines to memorize. Better get to work!

B. Feel uneasy. Why didn't you get a singing role when Diana and Katherine both did?

C. Are totally ticked off. You didn't get the part you wanted. Candace now thinks she's better than you, and Heather told you she's a star.

7. It's Tuesday morning and there is a brand-new zit on your chin. You…

A. Groan…then wash your face, clean the pimple, put on some medication and hope that no one notices it.

B. Groan…then wash your face, put on some medication and try to remember if anyone else in your class had new zits yesterday.

C. Groan…then wail, "I am the only one who ever gets zits. I am so ugly!"

8. Sonya, your partner for the history fair, asks if she can come over to your house so the two of you can work on your project. You…

A. Say, "Sure! Let me check with my dad to see when's a good time."

B. Say, "Uh, let me check with my dad." You are nervous about what Sonya may think of your house.

C. Say, "Let's work on the project at your house." You don't want Sonya to see where you live before you've seen where she lives–your house might not measure up.

✓ Check Your Answers

For each A answer give yourself 1 point, for each B answer 2 points, and for each C answer 3 points. Add up your total.

If you scored 8-12 points: You've learned that you are one-of-a-kind! You know that another person's yardstick can't measure you correctly. You're on the right track. Keep on being you!

If you scored 13-19 points: You may be using two yardsticks! While it is always good to consider others' opinions, it is not good to let their opinions drive your decisions. In the end, make sure that you make your own choices. Be yourself!

What does God have to say about that? Read on…

God Puts It This Way

No servant can serve two masters. Either he will hate the one and love the other, or he will be devoted to the one and despise the other.

~Luke 16:13

What God Means Is

Don't let your friends' opinions have more influence on your life than God's ideas.

If you scored 20-24 points: You are using someone else's yardstick! Don't continue to compare yourself to everybody else in order to decide that you are okay. Instead, decide first that you are okay because you are God's girl. Then, compare yourself to what He wants of you. In other words, use the yardstick He gives you. Be yourself!

God Puts It This Way

Am I now trying to win the approval of men, or of God? Or am I trying to please men?

~Galatians 1:10

Talk to God

Dear God, help me to know that I am okay because I am God's girl. I want to use the yardstick You have made especially for me. Show me how to do that today. Remind me when I start to play The Comparison Game the wrong way. Help me to be myself. In Jesus' name, Amen.

FAQs: There's Only 1 U

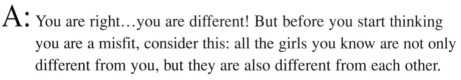

Different

Q: I feel like I am so different from other girls I know. Why would anyone want to be my friend?

A: You are right…you are different! But before you start thinking you are a misfit, consider this: all the girls you know are not only different from you, but they are also different from each other.

Picture a few of them in your mind. Consider…

✳ Looks: tall, short, blond, dark, redhead?

✳ Style: hip, retro, down-home, classic?

✳ Hobbies and interests: sports, dance, science, art, reading, music?

✳ Qualities: outgoing, quiet, fun-loving, serious?

✳ Character traits: responsible, caring, honest, fair, hard-working?

Each girl has her own unique "personality fingerprint" that is different from all the others. So you are in good company. Everyone is different!

Not Special

Q: How do I know I'm special? I don't feel special at all.

A: Wrongo! Nix! Not so! Untrue! No way!
Off the mark! God made you and He thinks you are very special. In fact, He says you are "wonderful"!

God Puts It This Way

I praise you because I am fearfully and wonderfully made; your works are wonderful.

~Psalm 139:14

You are not just one more replica God cranked out of His heavenly assembly line factory. No, He took special care to make a work of art when He created you.

God Puts It This Way

For you created my inmost being; you knit me together.

~Psalm 139:13

What God Means Is

He "knit" your body together and He created your soul. That makes you a handmade work of art. You are one-of-a-kind! There's only 1 U!

Oops!

Q: Sometimes people make things and when they are done, they don't like what they made. Could that be the case with God and me?

A: Nope! God not only likes everything He made, He loves everything He made.

God Puts It This Way

I have loved you with an everlasting love; I have drawn you with loving-kindness.

~Jeremiah 31:3

What God Means Is

God loves you forever and ever, no matter what. He created you the way He did because He loves you so much. God makes no mistakes!

Memo: Your Very Special Mission
To: You
From: The Friendship Coach
Subject: Your Very Special Mission

Dear (*your name*),

I have a Very Special Mission for you.

You may think that you are (*name a reason why you think no one would want to be your friend*).

But I see things differently. Instead, I see your inner self, (*your name*) - your unfading beauty and your gentle, quiet spirit, which is of great worth to Me (1 Peter 3:4).

You, (*your name*), are precious and honored in My sight, and I love you. I will give others in exchange for you, (*your name*), and people in exchange for your life (Isaiah 43:4). Never forget, (*your name*), that I have called you by name, and you are mine! (Isaiah 43:1).

There is only 1 U. I have placed you in a specific group of friends for a purpose. When you show compassion and caring to a friend, you are actually showing her that I, God, love her. When you laugh and have fun with your friends, you are demonstrating My joy - the joy of the Lord.

Therefore, this is your Very Special Mission: I am counting on you to reflect My love in the world in your own unique way.

Your Very Special Mission is also recorded in the Bible.

Let's put it this way: "We are therefore Christ's ambassadors, as though God were making his appeal through us" (2 Corinthians 5:20).

Love,

The Lord God Almighty

♪ A Note to Myself

Today's date: _____

I am marking this page in a special way and I will refer to it when I need a reminder of my Very Special Mission.

QUIZ! That's My Friendship Style

When it comes to being with your friends, what's your style? Circle the letter next to each statement that sounds most like you.

1. A group of girls decides to meet at the community center to play ping-pong.

A. You're the one who contacts the center and reserves the game room. Then you call and invite everyone you know to come.

B. Rebecca reserves the game room and calls to tell you about it. You offer to help her organize the get-together.

C. Two hours of ping-pong was a blast. You make a point to thank Rebecca for making all the arrangements.

2. The school band sponsors a car wash to raise money for a trip to an amusement park.

A. You are student-in-charge: you make certain there is enough soap, buckets, sponges, student workers and adult helpers.

B. You work hard with a team of three other band members and wash 12 cars.

C. You encourage other band members by relieving them when they need a break.

3 Brooke gets knocked down during the field hockey game.

A. You alert the referee and immediately tell the coach and trainer what you saw happen to Brooke.

B. You pass the word to the other athletes on the field so that everyone knows what is going on.

C. You are at Brooke's side instantly, giving her reassurance, and you assist her off the field.

4 Sandi has surgery.

A. You create a schedule so that one friend will call Sandi each day.

B. You participate in the "I'll call Sandi" schedule. You sign up to call her on Thursday, and you do it.

C. You call Sandi on Thursday and find out she's discouraged. You call back Friday, just to see if she's OK.

5 Brianna interrupts Caitlyn during lunch.

A. A friend war between Brianna and Caitlyn erupts. You say, "Come on, this is not a big deal. Let's get over it."

B. You notice the friend war is about to erupt. You try to diffuse it by stepping in with, "Caitlyn, what were you saying?"

C. When Caitlyn starts crying, you put your arm around her.

 Check Your Answers

If you circled mostly A's...

You motivate and mobilize others! You are enthusiastic. People enjoy being around you and you enjoy them. You are a leader.

 Use It

Keep an eye out for friends who are shy and not as outgoing as you.

Help them feel included by inviting them to join in all the fun.

 ## Be Careful

It's easy to get so caught up in your social life that you find you don't have enough time for God. Make time to be alone with Him, too!

If you circled mostly B's...

You are a team player! You find ways to work well with others for the good of the larger group. Others know they can count on you to be capable and reliable, and to do what you say you will do.

Did You Know?

A Bible character known for being a leader who motivated and mobilized others was ?, the Christian church's first missionary. (Check your answer on page 185.)

 ## Use It

Be sure to use your "all-for-one" spirit to keep your own relationships in good order. Be on the lookout for chances to diffuse conflict with tact.

 ## Be Careful

Use your peacemaking skills when you can, but remember that you cannot fix every skirmish you see. Sometimes you must step back and let others resolve their differences!

Did You Know?

A Bible character known for recruiting others to "join the team" was ?, the disciple who introduced Simon Peter to Jesus. (Answer on page 185.)

If you circled mostly C's...

Encouragement is your middle name! You are a supportive and sensitive friend. You care about other people and you show that concern in real ways.

 ## Use It

Look for ways to affirm others, especially those who are having a rough day. Everyone from the most outspoken leader to the quietest bookworm appreciates kindness.

 ## Be Careful

When a giving person thinks she must "buy" or "earn" friends, her thoughtfulness is less genuine. Make sure that your acts of kindness have no strings attached.

Did You Know?

A Bible character known for being an encourager was ?, a deacon in the early Christian church, whose name means "Son of Encouragement" (Check your answer on page 185.)

A Tip from The Friendship Coach

You may be a leader in youth chorus, be a team player on the volleyball court, and an encourager to the girls in your neighborhood. Everyone plays different roles in different friendships at different times. Ask God what role He wants you take on in the different areas of your life!

 ## Talk to God

Dear God, I feel like You've given me a gift to be (name which style you think is your strong suit). But I know that I can be a leader, a team player and an encourager with my friends at different times. Thank You that all three friendship styles are important. Show me which way to be a friend today. In Jesus' name, Amen.

● Make It! ● There's Only 1 U Mirror

··

This mirror has magnets on the back. You can hang it inside a metal locker at school, in the gym or on any other metal surface. Each time you look in your **There's Only 1 U Mirror** you'll remember how special you are. Plus, it will remind you of your very special mission: you are to reflect God's love to your friends.

 ## What You Need

✳ CD (or small mirror)
✳ newspapers
✳ paint pens
✳ small rhinestones or sequins
✳ glitter glue
✳ craft glue
✳ adhesive-backed magnet strips
✳ ruler
✳ scissors

What to Do

1. Spread newspapers over your work surface. Lay the CD flat with the shiniest side facing up.

2. Use paint pens to write "There's Only 1 U" around the center hole of the compact disc.

3. Decorate the outside edge of the CD with glitter glue, rhinestones, sequins and paint pens. Allow your newly decorated mirror to dry completely.

4. Cut four ½" pieces from the magnet strip. Attach the magnets to the back of your new mirror.

5. Hang your new **There's Only 1 U Mirror** in your locker or on a metal surface.

Hint: Some CDs are more reflective than others. Be sure to check your image in the CD before you select it for this project.

Chapter Four

Finding & Making Friends

"I know that [God] can do all things;
no plan of [His] can be thwarted."

~Job 42:2

❋ What You Absolutely, Positively ❋ Need to Know First

...about finding and making friends

What you may be thinking

You are the only one in the entire universe who feels anxious about making friends.

What you may not be thinking

(but can be very helpful to know)

❋ Every girl wants to make friends.

❋ Every girl is worried she won't.

❋ Every girl around you is nervous about how to do it.

❋ Every girl is afraid of looking like a complete fool.

❋ Every girl appreciates someone who is friendly to her.

What you absolutely, positively need to know

✳ You do not have to do this alone–you are God's girl!

✳ You have **The Friendship Coach** to help you.

✳ You can talk to the **Coach** anytime–even when others are around.

✳ You can know that the **Coach** understands better than anyone.

✳ You can ask the **Coach** for the next play.

✳ You can rely on the **Coach** to give you courage.

God Puts It This Way

Do not fear, for I am with you; do not be dismayed, for I am your God. I will strengthen you and help you; I will uphold you with my righteous right hand.

~Isaiah 41:10

Talk to God

Dear God, right now I am afraid or nervous about making friends because (say why and describe your feelings). But You promise in Isaiah 41:10 that You will be with me, strengthen me, help me and uphold me. I am taking You at Your word. Show me how to make friends and how to handle my feelings. I trust You. In Jesus' name, Amen.

Write About It

Re-read Isaiah 41:10. Write a list of all God's promises for you in this passage!

_____

_____

_____

♪ A Note to Myself

Today's date: _____.

Re-read this entry on _____. Think about how God is helping you! Make sure you thank Him for keeping His promises.

FAQs: Where to Look

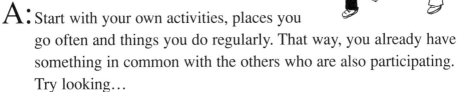

Where Do I Start?

Q: I want to make some friends, but I am not sure where to look.

A: Start with your own activities, places you go often and things you do regularly. That way, you already have something in common with the others who are also participating. Try looking…

✳ In your neighborhood or at the community center.

✳ On the bus or on the way to school.

✳ In class or at home-school gatherings.

✳ At sports practice or club meetings.

✳ At youth group or at church.

✳ In the car pool or at after-school activities.

Something in Common

Q: Why does it help to have something in common with a new friend?

A: Remember this? It's from The Friendship Top 10: "A friend makes doing things as two more fun than one." Looking for friends as you go about your regular activities makes sense because you have some important things already built in to your friendship. You already have…

✳ Similar schedules (you already spend time together).

✳ Similar responsibilities (you have the same homework).

✳ Similar interests (you like ballet).

That will give you and your new friend things to talk about, someone with whom to share those things and someone with whom to grow!

I'm Not Sure

Q: How do I know that there are friends out there for me?

A: Talk to **The Friendship Coach!** He will assure you. After all, He already knows who will be friends with whom!

 ## God Puts It This Way

I know that [God] can do all things; no plan of [His] can be thwarted.
                                                    ~Job 42:2

 ## Talk to God

Dear God, thank You that You already know who my friends will be. Show me where to look for them. Point them out to me and help me see who I should get to know. In Jesus' name, Amen.

Real Girl TIPS

"I realize that making new friends is awkward for both of us. I try to act as normal as I can."

Yolanda, age 12
North Carolina

Icebreakers: 10 Easy Ways to Start a Conversation

❋ Introduce yourself.

❋ Find out about her family.

❋ Play "favorites." (For example: "What's your favorite TV show?")

❋ Ask about her weekend or vacation.

❋ Ask about her hobbies.

❋ Point out a connection.

❋ Invite her to join you.

❋ Pay her a compliment.

❋ Ask her opinion.

❋ Talk about the weather!

QUIZ! Help! I'm Really Shy

Circle true or false.

1 I am the only one who feels shy.

    True   **False**

2 "She's not shy–she's stuck up!" is always true.

    True   **False**

3 "Shy" means the same thing as "not confident."

    True   **False**

4 Shy girls never have a lot of friends.

True   False

5 I'm shy, and there's no way I can ever learn to get over it.

True   False

✔ Check your answers!

1. **False.** Everyone feels shy from time to time. Even outgoing girls sometimes consider themselves shy, or can be overwhelmed by a noisy, talkative group. With practice, anyone can develop the confidence to reach out and make the first move.

2. **False.** One pitfall of being shy is being mistaken for being arrogant. "I saw Amanda point to me and whisper to Jessica, 'She's so stuck up!'" shared one shy girl. "I pretended not to notice, but I felt terrible. I don't think I'm better than anyone–I'm just shy." Most shy girls don't talk as much as others do. There are ways to get around this: smile, nod and make eye contact with other girls when you don't feel like talking.

Real Girl TIPS

"I find out as soon as possible what is similar between us. Then we have something to talk about."

Rita, age 10
Alaska

3. **False.** "Shy" is not a synonym for "unconfident." A shy person can be quiet, reserved, private and restrained–and she can also be confident in knowing that God gave her these gentle strengths.

4. **False.** Quiet, thoughtful girls are usually sensitive as well. These types usually make many lasting friendships because they are considerate of other people's feelings.

5. **False.** Go back to the 10 Icebreakers on page 59 to figure out ways you can be the one to break the ice and start a conversation!

This Is Taking Forever

It's easy to get discouraged and frustrated when you are trying so hard to make friends. Make sure you have realistic expectations.

Realistic Expectation #1: Making friends takes time.

You can't just meet a fun person, sprinkle her with Super-Fantastic-Instantaneous-Friend Fairy Dust, tap her on the forehead with your Wonderful-Friend-to-Be Wand and poof–have a fantastic friend. Be patient.

"After I get to know a new friend, I ask her if she'd like to go to the park or come to my house."

Summer, age 10
Pennsylvania

Realistic Expectation #2: You will make some mistakes.

UUUGGGHHH! But maybe you are unaware that mistakes can be turned into advantages if you think about them the right way:

Advantage A: After you make a mistake, you can recover. Then you will realize that learning from your mistake can make you smarter.

Advantage B: After someone else makes a mistake, you may get hurt. You can recover. Then you will realize that someone else's mistake can make you stronger.

Advantage C: Because you can learn from your mistakes and everyone else's, you can avoid making the same mistake twice. Then you will realize that mistakes can make you grow.

God Puts It This Way

We know that in all things God works for the good of those who love him.

~Romans 8:28

Realistic Expectation #3: It's easy to get discouraged and give up. Don't do it!

God Puts It This Way

Let us not become weary in doing good, for at the proper time we will reap a harvest if we do not give up.

~Galatians 6:9

What God Means

Keep trying. God promises you will reap a fantastic friendship harvest when you stick with it, doing things His way.

Talk to God

Dear God, I am sorry that I get discouraged and frustrated about making friends. You can tell that I am trying very hard. I want to stick with it and not give up. I trust that You are making me into the kind of friend You want me to be. In Jesus' name, Amen.

Real Girl TIPS

"Jokes, humor, funny faces–I do things to make both of us laugh."

Laurie, age 11
New Mexico

Make It! Circle of Friends Phone Flipper

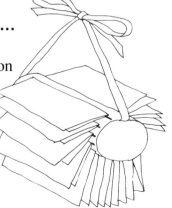

Invite a new friend to join you for an afternoon of crafts! Each of you can make your own **Circle of Friends Phone Flipper**. Record your new friend's name, phone number, address, e-mail address and birthday on the first card you put in your flipper.

What You Need

- ❋ toilet tissue tube
- ❋ ruler
- ❋ 3" x 5" index cards
- ❋ markers
- ❋ stickers
- ❋ strand of yarn, 2 yards

- ❋ colorful paper (construction paper or gift wrap)
- ❋ ½"-wide ribbon, 1 yard
- ❋ clear packaging tape, 2" wide
- ❋ acid-free scrapbooking glue
- ❋ scissors

What to Do

1. To make the flipper base, cut a 5½" square of colorful paper. Apply acid-free scrapbooking glue to one side of the paper. Attach the paper to the toilet tissue tube, overlapping the paper edges where they meet on the outside of the tube. Turn and attach the paper ends to the inside of the tube.

2. Cut three lengths of clear packaging tape. Apply it to the paper-covered tube, turning the tape ends to the inside of the tube.

3. Make 18 cuts, ¼" deep and about ¼" apart, around each end of the tube. Be sure to make the same number of cuts in both tube ends.

4. Leave a 1" tail of yarn inside the tube and secure the strand in one of the notches. Thread the yarn back and forth across the outside of the Flipper, securing the yarn firmly in each ¼" notch and pulling it taut. Continue weaving the yarn until all the notches are threaded. Tie the yarn ends together. Trim and discard the excess.

5. Fold the index cards in half. On the outside of each card, write a friend's name. Use the inside of the card to record your friend's phone number, street address, e-mail address and birthday. Decorate the cards with markers and stickers. Hook the cards through the yarn strands. Adjust the cards alphabetically.

6. Thread the ½" ribbon through the flipper. Tie the ribbon ends in a bow. Hang the flipper in a special place.

7. Keep track of your new friends with your new **Circle of Friends Phone Flipper**!

Chapter Five

Be a Fantastic Friend

"Love your neighbor as yourself."

~James 2:8

✳ A ★ ★ ★ ★ Friend ✳

Loyalty. Trustworthiness. Consideration. A Good Listener. A girl who demonstrates these qualities stands way above the crowd. She earns the title, "4★ Friend." See if you can match up each 4★ quality below to one of the descriptions that follow.

4★ loyalty   4★ trustworthiness

4★ consideration   4★ a good listener

1. You became friends with Lindsey three years ago at church. Other kids teased her because she uses a wheelchair, but you think she is a lot of fun. You attend a public school, and Lindsey is home-schooled, but you still spend a lot of time together making things, talking about books and listening to music. Even though you are involved in sports and Lindsey isn't, her friendship is important to you.

   You show this special mark of a 4★ friend: _____.

2. Angela just told you that her father moved out of the house last week and her parents are going to get a divorce. "I know I can trust you not to tell anyone," she says. "I won't tell anyone," you promise. "I'll keep your secret." Five minutes later, Jordan taps you on the shoulder. "What's Angela so upset about?" she demands to know. You answer, "She just needs some privacy."

   You show this special mark of a 4★ friend: _____.

3. Joani started coming to your scout club meetings this week. At craft time, you notice that she does not have a partner. You remember how left out you felt at your first few meetings. You walk over to Joani, introduce yourself and ask, "Would you like to be my partner?" Joani gives you a big smile and says, "That would be great!"

   You show this special mark of a 4★ friend: _____.

4. In the lunchroom, you notice that Corinne ignores Tanya. Tanya's face gets red and she turns her head away. You sit down next to Tanya and say, "You must feel badly. Do you want to talk about it?" You listen carefully and let Tanya talk about her hurt feelings.

You show this special mark of a 4★ friend: _____.

Here's how the answers line up:

1. Loyalty   2. Trustworthiness

3. Consideration   4. A good listener

Read on to learn more about 4★ qualities of a fantastic friend!

Loyalty

Loyalty shows faithfulness. Loyal friends stay friends for a long time. When you're loyal, you find ways to appreciate your friend even though she may be different from you.

 Use It

Be on the lookout for someone who needs a friend. Lots of girls don't feel close to anybody–they may have recently moved to the community, their parents may be distracted by work or they may not have a church home. Use your ability to cultivate deep friendships and connect with someone new.

"One of us has to make the first move. I figure it may as well be me. So I introduce myself and start talking."

Alisha, age 12
Illinois

 Be Careful

It's easy to think that a couple of close friends are all you need. Once in awhile, your best buds may find other friends. Encourage them rather than getting jealous.

The Loyal-o-meter!

Just like you check the thermometer for a temperature, you can check the Loyal-o-meter to find out if you are being a fickle, wishy-washy or loyal friend. Check out the Loyal-o-meter ratings below, then read the stories and find out how they rate on the Loyal-o-meter.

Loyal-o-meter Ratings:

★ or less: Fickle and flighty! Loyalty means liking your friend for who she is, no matter who is around.

★↗ to ★★↗ : Wishy-washy! Friendships change. But don't get swayed away from a friend just because your schedules don't completely line up or you're involved in different kinds of activities. If someone is a terrific friend, make it a point to keep it that way.

★★★ to ★★★★★: A loyal friend! All friends disagree from time to time, but loyal friends make up after an argument. And a loyal friend is someone who sticks with you–both during exciting times when you get a lot of attention, and in the hard times when you feel all alone.

You and Lizzie are talking about your favorite nail polish when all of a sudden The Popular Kids walk by. You turn away and pretend you don't know Lizzie.
Loyal-o-meter rating: ↗

You and Amber have been close friends since you were in the first grade. But this year, Amber is home-schooled, which is frustrating for you. Amber doesn't "get" what's going on with the crowd at school, so you don't spend much time talking with her anymore.
Loyal-o-meter rating: ★↗

You were selected for the dance troupe but Shannon was not. She was hurt when you started spending more time with the other dancers, but how can you help it when you have rehearsals? You'll make it up to her. Now that dance season is over, you are seeing more of Shannon. She seems happy and uneasy at the same time.

Loyal-o-meter rating: ★ ★

After your food fight, you and Dana can't stop laughing even though you both were sent to the principal's office. In fact, you help Dana pick the cherry gelatin out of her ponytail.

Loyal-o-meter rating: ★ ★ ★

Jolene is running for student council and you've been her staunchest supporter. You put up posters, ask all your friends to vote for her and remind her about her great speech at the candidate debate. Jolene loses the election, but you're still her friend.

Loyal-o-meter rating: ★ ★ ★ ★

 ## God Puts It This Way
A faithful man will be richly blessed.

~Proverbs 28:20

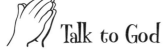 ## Talk to God

Dear God, thank You for my friend (name a loyal friend) who stuck by me when (name a time when your friend was loyal). I am not sure I am being loyal to (name a friend) when (name a situation). Show me how to be a faithful friend to her today. In Jesus' name, Amen.

Trustworthiness

Trustworthiness shows you are a friend who can be counted on. Trustworthy friends do what they say they will do, and they can be trusted to keep a secret. If you are trustworthy, you are reliable, consistent and dependable.

 ## Use It

Everyone needs a friend to trust. Be that kind of friend to those around you.

 ## Be Careful

A trustworthy reputation is earned over time. Don't make the mistake of squandering it when you have the urge to share someone else's "big news."

 ## Spotlight on...

Trustworthy Tammy and Unpredictable Paula

Let Trustworthy Tammy and Unpredictable Paula show you how important trustworthiness can be.

Trustworthy Tammy

- ✳ Meets you at 6:00, just as she promised.
- ✳ Remembers to bring the CD you wanted to borrow.
- ✳ RSVPs to your party invitation on time.
- ✳ Stays late to help you decorate for the Harvest Festival.
- ✳ Answers her e-mail.
- ✳ Thanks your mom for giving her a ride.
- ✳ Shows up to church every week.

✳ Knows the date of her harp recital and is preparing for it now.

✳ Finds out who will be going to the party before she asks her parents for permission.

✳ Keeps your crush on Thomas a secret.

Unpredictable Paula

✳ Shows up late…if at all.

✳ Forgets to tell you she can't give you a ride.

✳ Leaves her backpack at your house (and doesn't realize it for 2 weeks).

✳ Calls every night to get the math homework assignment.

✳ Borrows your jacket without asking you.

✳ Doesn't know her dad's phone number at work.

✳ Cancels her trombone lesson to go to the mall.

✳ Oversleeps the Sunday morning she has nursery duty at church.

✳ Can't find the directions to Cynthia's house.

✳ Blabs about your crush on Thomas to the entire school.

Real Girl TIPS

"Courtney is my best friend. I can tell her my secrets and she doesn't laugh–or tell anyone. I can always get an honest opinion from her, too."

Mary, age 10
Maryland

The Tale of the Secret

Part of being a trustworthy friend is knowing when and how to keep a secret. Read on to see if Bobbi is a trustworthy friend to Kristy.

Monday 8:22 am
At the bus stop, Kristy confides to Bobbi, "My parents just told me we are going to move to New Zealand. I don't want to go. Please don't tell anybody." Bobbi agrees to keep Kristy's secret.

Monday 8:47 am
The bus arrives at school. Bobbi sees Erin walking into the building and runs over to her. "Kristy is moving to New Zealand this summer," she says to Erin. "Don't tell anyone. It's a secret." Erin agrees to keep it a secret.

Monday 10:10 am
"It might be winter here," says Mrs. Shelton, the social studies teacher, "but in the southern hemisphere, people in New Zealand and Australia are finishing up their summer holidays and getting ready to head back to school." Erin leans over to Tess and whispers, "Kristy is moving to New Zealand in June when it will be winter there. I heard it's because her parents don't want to take any more summer vacations. But don't tell anyone. It's a secret." Tess agrees to keep it a secret.

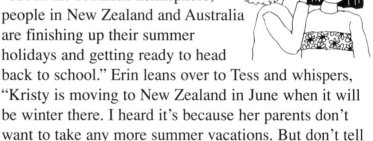

Monday 11:45 am
"Are you going out for the softball team, Kristy?" Megan asks on the way to gym class. Tess pulls Megan aside. "Kristy was so upset last year that she didn't make the team," Tess says, "that her parents decided to move to New Zealand. They're leaving in

April to avoid softball season. But keep it to yourself." Megan agrees to keep it a secret.

Monday 2:18 pm

Kristy looks at the C+ grade on her math test and sighs. Megan notices, and leans over to Danielle. "Kristy is moving to New Zealand at the end of this semester," Megan says quietly. "Her parents think the schools are better over there. Don't tell anyone." Danielle agrees to keep it a secret.

Monday 3:25 pm

At the bus stop, Danielle sees Kristy. "Call me tonight and I will help you with the math homework, okay? Then you might not need to move to New Zealand!" Kristy is confused. Why did Danielle offer to help her with math? Today was the first time she received a score lower than an A. And how did she know about New Zealand?

Monday 3:29 pm

Megan sits down next to Kristy on the bus. "I just know you'll make the softball team this year," Megan says. "Promise me you'll try out. I don't want you to move to New Zealand!" Kristy is bewildered. When she didn't get on the softball team last spring, she signed up for soccer, had a blast, and plans to do it again. And what does that have to with New Zealand?

Monday 3:33 pm

Erin pulls Kristy aside. "I'm going to ask my mom if you can come with us to the beach in August. That way your parents won't have to worry about taking summer vacations. And you won't have to move to New Zealand!" Kristy is confused. Her parents were already planning a camping trip to the Smoky Mountains in August. And there's that New Zealand thing again!

Monday
3:56 pm
Kristy and Bobbi get off the bus. "There's a For Sale sign in front of your house, Kristy!" says Bobbi. Kristy finally realizes what happened. She looks at Bobbi in complete frustration. "I already told you, Bobbi. We're moving to that new neighborhood in the suburbs called New Zealand. But we have to sell our house first."

The Secret to Keeping Secrets

Keeping Secrets Rule 1: If you tell one person a secret, chances are it won't remain a secret for long. People like to feel they know more than others. The urge to share insider knowledge is more tempting than the commitment to keep it quiet.

Keeping Secrets Rule 2: As more people share your secret, the secret changes and grows. People make assumptions when they match a secret with a person. They add those assumptions onto the secret when they pass it along.

Keeping Secrets Rule 3: When you promise to keep a secret, but then pass it along, someone always gets hurt. Who gets hurt? It could be person who had the secret. It could be someone else who is mentioned in the secret. It could be someone who hears the secret. Or it could be you, the secret teller. When you don't keep your word, you become less trustworthy. You have broken a vow. And that always hurts who you are and who you will become.

Did You Know?

There was a woman in the Bible who kept the secret that she was one of God's people. Later she became a queen and saved the Jewish nation. What was her name? See page 185 for the answer.

Keeping Secrets Rule 4: This one is simple: keep your word!

God Puts It This Way

A gossip betrays a confidence, but a trustworthy man keeps a secret.

~Proverbs 11:13

Talk to God

Dear God, I admit it: I like hearing secrets from other people! The problem is that I also like to pass them along to other friends. I confess to You that I did this when (name a time when you promised to keep a secret, but didn't). Help me to change this part of me. Help me to be trustworthy. In Jesus' name, Amen.

A Note to Myself

Mark this page a special way. Turn back to it each time you hear a secret and want to make sure you keep it.

Consideration

Consideration reveals your kindness and thoughtfulness. A considerate friend is sensitive to other people's feelings. To be considerate, demonstrate that you care about your friends in real ways.

Use It

Look for chances to be considerate! Everybody, no matter how self-confident they seem, appreciates kindness and thoughtfulness.

Be Careful

Make sure that your acts of consideration have no strings attached. If a giving person thinks she must buy or earn friends, her kindness is less genuine.

QUIZ! How Considerate of You!

Showing consideration doesn't take much effort. But tiny bits of consideration can turn you into a 4★ Friend! Circle the answer below that shows how you would be the most considerate friend.

1. You and Stephanie just finished having a sandwich at her house. You…

A. Rinse off the dishes, load them in the dishwasher, put the sandwich meat back in the refrigerator and thank Stephanie's mom for the snack.

B. Throw everything in the sink and yell, "See you later!" to Stephanie's mom as you race up to Stephanie's room.

C. Eat–and then run outside to play basketball.

2. The fire alarm rings during science class. It may be a drill, but then again, it may not be. You…

A. Move quickly toward the door, but grow impatient because Nicole is taking f-o-r-e-v-e-r.

B. Elbow your way past Christopher, Matthew and Kevin to make a pathway for Nicole.

C. Offer to help Nicole with her crutches.

3. You're at crafts club. Monica stands up suddenly and knocks over an entire carton of beads. They fly everywhere. You…

A. Snicker and say, "Way to go, Monica!" as you continue to put the finishing touches on your necklace.

B. Sigh, roll your eyes, and say, "I'll move out of your way so you can clean up your mess."

C. Smile to Monica and say, "That could happen to anyone. Let me help you pick them up."

4. For the first time, identical twins Mary and Jean have on different outfits. Jean's seat is next to yours. You say…

A. "Why did you wear that today? Now you can't play tricks on everyone."

B. "I love your skirt. Blue looks good on you."

C. "At last! What made you finally decide to be yourselves? Everyone was beginning to wonder about you."

5. Allie hasn't been to youth group in two weeks. You…

A. Call and tell her you've missed her.

B. Don't even notice her absence.

C. Think to yourself, *She must be such a snob to miss two weeks and not tell anyone.*

> ✓ RACHAEL
> ✓ CARMEN
> ALLIE
> ✓ ELIZABETH
> ✓ THERESA
> ✓ TARA

6. Emma won't be able to attend the youth rally on Saturday because she doesn't have a ride. "Oh, I really wish I could go!" she says. You…

A. Say, "That's really too bad. I hear the bands are going to be awesome."

B. Say, "Why can't your mom take the day off work so you can go?"

C. Check with your parents, and then tell Emma, "We can give you a ride if it's okay with your mom."

Check your answers!

1. A. How considerate of you! You cleaned up after yourself rather than letting Stephanie's mom be your maid, and you thanked her rather than running off rudely. You showed respect for your friend's parents and her personal belongings.

2. C. How considerate of you! In a pressured situation, you kept your cool. Instead of being impatient or impolite, you were sensitive to a classmate who needed extra help.

3. C. How considerate of you! Rather than making fun of Monica's clumsiness or moaning about the messy inconvenience, you put her feelings first. You expressed understanding that she might feel badly–and then offered to help her.

4. B. How considerate of you! Rather than pelting Jean with questions about the change, you showed respect for her individuality. Moreover, everyone appreciates a sincere compliment.

5. A. How considerate of you! Not only did you notice Allie's absence, but you also took the time and effort to check on her. You demonstrated compassion rather than selfishness or a judgmental attitude.

6. C. How considerate of you! You knew Emma already felt badly about missing the rally, so you didn't put it ahead of other important things in her life (such as her mom's job). Instead, you found a way to include her. You also showed responsibility by asking for permission before you made any promises.

God Puts It This Way

Whoever can be trusted with very little can also be trusted with much, and whoever is dishonest with very little will also be dishonest with much.

~Luke 16:10

What God Means

Small acts of kindness show a heart growing in God's love.

Talk to God

Dear God, I want to show consideration to at least one person, at least once each day, in just one small way. Show me who that person should be today–and what You want me to do. In Jesus' name, Amen.

● Make It! ● Tiny Kindness Box

A small box of kindness is more than enough.
A little goes a long, long way.
Notice a friend who needs a surprise
And give her some kindness today!

This little box takes only minutes to put together. Make several at a time. Give them to friends to show them that you care!

What You Need

✳ gift wrap or other brightly-colored paper

✳ ⅛" wide satin ribbon

✳ scissors

✳ ruler

✳ pencil

✳ tape

✳ craft glue

✳ a tiny note

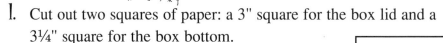

What to Do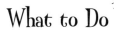

1. Cut out two squares of paper: a 3" square for the box lid and a 3¼" square for the box bottom.

2. On the wrong side of the paper, measure and mark the center of each square with an "x" (Diagram A).

Diagram A

78

3. Make either the lid or the bottom first: one at a time, fold each point of the square into the center so that it touches the middle of the "x." Do not unfold (Diagram B).

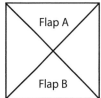

Diagram B

4. Fold two parallel sides of the square so that they just barely touch in the center of the square. These will form the sides of the box (Diagram C-1). Repeat this procedure for the other two remaining parallel sides (Diagram C-2).

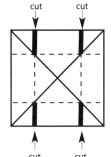

Diagram C-1

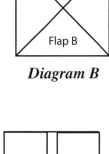

Diagram C-2

5. Unfold the square so it looks like Diagram B again. Clip along the folds where the thick lines are in Diagram D.

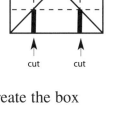

Diagram D

6. Open up Flap A (see Diagram B). Fold up Sides A and B, then fold Flap A down over both side corners. Do the same with Flap B to create the box (Diagram E).

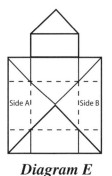

7. Once all four corners are folded securely, tape the paper points in the center.

Diagram E

8. Repeat steps 3-7 for the other box part.

9. With the satin ribbon, tie a tiny bow. Glue bow onto the box lid.

10. Place a tiny note, such as "UR Special" or "I'm your friend" in your **Tiny Kindness Box**.

11. Give the box to a friend or hide it in a place where she will be sure to find it!

A Good Listener

A good listener is a friend who cares enough to listen. Instead of always being the one who has to talk, make others feel comfortable enough to share what they think.

 ## Use It

Keep your eyes open for friends who may appear lonely, shy or depressed. You can offer them a caring, listening ear.

 ## Be Careful

Even though you are always willing to listen to someone else's point of view, remember that you can have your own ideas, too. It is okay to have a different opinion than someone else.

FAQs: How to Grow Your Ears

Be Genuinely Interested

Q: Brenda asked, "How did your soccer game go?" I began explaining, but then I noticed that she wasn't paying attention. I don't want to be like that. I want my friends to feel like they're important to me. What can I do?

A: There is nothing more annoying than a friend who asks you a question and then doesn't listen to your answer. You wonder...

❋ Does she really want to know how the game went?

❋ Why are her eyes glazing over?

❋ Why did she only say "Uh-huh" when I described my breakaway and assist in the third quarter?

✳ Why did she ask if she is not even looking at me?

You get that nagging feeling that she is not really interested!

So when you ask a friend about her game (or whatever you ask)…

✳ Look her in the eye. Even if you aren't interested in soccer, you are still interested in your friend.

✳ Follow the conversation.

✳ Ask about details you don't understand. In other words…be genuinely interested!

Follow Up

Q: On Friday, I asked Jeni what she was doing over the weekend. She told me she was going to her dad's house. Then on Monday when I asked her what she did over the weekend, she said, "Duh, I went to my dad's house!" I felt badly. What should I have asked instead?

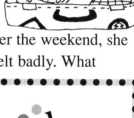

A: You learned an important lesson about being a good listener. Not only should you listen at the time you ask the question, you should also follow up. Following up can be a little trickier than just asking a question, however. Here's how to do it:

✳ Ask or talk to a friend about her interests or plans.

✳ As you listen, make a mental note of what is really important to her. ("I'm nervous about my book report on Tuesday" or "My neighbor is interviewing me tomorrow for a babysitting job.")

interviewing me tomorrow for a babysitting job.")

✳ Ask about it the next time you see her. ("How did your book report go?" or "Did you get that babysitting job?")

Real Girl TIPS

"I ask a new friend questions. Also, I talk about myself a bit, so things aren't one-sided. Pretty soon we feel comfortable with each other."

Shamika, age 12
Virginia

Following up shows you not only listened to your friend, it also shows that you care.

Give and Take

Q: Marissa always listens to me but I never feel like she understands how I feel. I don't want to do that to people, so how can I show them I understand what they're feeling?

A: It is just as frustrating to have a friend who doesn't reveal anything about herself as it is to have a friend who does all the talking. One of the best things about having a friend listen to you is you feel like you are not alone. So the next time you are listening to a friend share something, say, "I've felt that way before" or "I know exactly what you mean." This is called "give and take."

Listen Between the Lines

Q: Three girls used to pick on Shavonne at lunchtime. One day I asked her, "Do you feel better now that they moved to a different table?" She said, "Sure." But I think she was still a little uncomfortable. What should I have said or done?

A: A good listener hears not only the specific words but also hears the feelings behind those words. A good listener also notices clues. This is called "listening between the lines." Even though Shavonne claimed she felt better, you noticed how she hung her head and turned away. As a good listener (and friend) you should have offered to sit with Shavonne to take her mind off the bullies.

Talk to God

Dear God, You are such a good listener. You are genuinely interested in what I say to you. I know You care about me and what is on my mind, even if I don't use words to explain myself. Help me be that kind of caring listener with my friends. Give me an opportunity today to listen to my friends with my heart. In Jesus' name, Amen.

Real Girl TIPS

"I include a new friend in conversations and activities. That way she knows that I like her right from the start."

Lisa, age 11
Florida

● Make It! ● 4★Friend Shoelaces

Make these fun shoelaces to remind you how to be a 4★ friend! Make a pair for a friend, too.

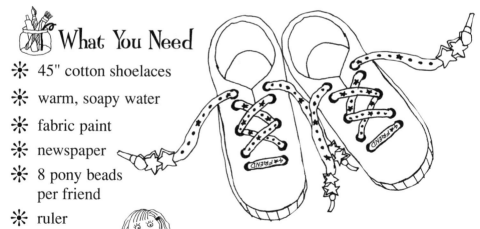

What You Need

※ 45" cotton shoelaces
※ warm, soapy water
※ fabric paint
※ newspaper
※ 8 pony beads per friend
※ ruler

What to Do

1. Prepare the shoelaces by washing them in warm, soapy water. Rinse the laces and allow them to dry completely.

2. Spread newspapers over your work area.

3. Lay the dry shoelaces flat. With a ruler, locate the center of the length of each shoelace. Using a thin bead of fabric paint, decorate the center 2" of each shoelace with "★ ★ ★ ★ Friend." Decorate the remainder of that side of each shoelace with stars and patterns as desired, leaving 2" undecorated at the ends for the beads. Allow the paint to dry completely.

4. Turn over the laces. Paint the opposite sides as desired, again leaving 2" undecorated at the ends for beads. Allow the paint to dry completely.

5. Thread the shoelaces through the eyes of the shoes, adjusting so "★ ★ ★ ★ Friend" stretches across the top of the shoe.

6. String pony beads onto the ends of the shoelaces. Tie a small knot at the end of the shoelaces to secure the beads.

Real Girl TIPS

"A popular person is kind and caring to everybody. That's why lots of people like her!"

Jessica, age 12
Maryland

Chapter Six

Best Buds

"My command is this: Love each other as I have loved you."

~John 15:12

❋ From Close to Closer ❋

You and a friend don't simply wake up one day and poof!–you are best buds. Here's how good friends move from being close to closer.

1. **Time.** You grow closer to a friend when you spend time with her.

❋ Over time, you find out things about each other that you never knew.

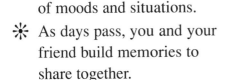

❋ You see each other in all kinds of moods and situations.

❋ As days pass, you and your friend build memories to share together.

2. **Circumstances.** You grow closer to a friend when you share both good and bad times.

❋ Your friend's support during a hard time makes you feel less lonely.

❋ Your friend's joy for you increases your happiness.

3. **Trust.** You grow closer to a friend as you earn and learn trust.

❋ Trust is earned. You earn your friend's trust when you keep your word the first time–and keep it the next time, and the next.

❋ Trust is learned. You learn your friend can be trusted when she keeps her word the first time–and the next time, and the next.

God Puts It This Way

My command is this: Love each other as I have loved you.

~John 15:12

Talk to God

Dear God, thank You for my best friend (name). Help me grow closer to her by being the kind of friend that pleases you. In Jesus' name, Amen.

QUIZ! Facts About Best Friends

Having a best bud can be fun, exhilarating… and frustrating, if you are not prepared. Get the facts straight to prevent confusion about "best friends." Circle the answer you think is best, then turn to the page to find out the facts.

1. "Best friend" is just another way of saying "super-close friend." It doesn't necessarily mean "the only kind of friend worth having."

   True   **Not true**

2. If you have a best friend, you must spend all your time with her, and no one else.

   True   **Not true**

3. It's possible to have other "best friends" in addition to your best bud.

   True   **Not true**

4. You can't be best friends with every person you know.

   True   **Not true**

5. Your best friend will never hurt you.

   True   **Not true**

87

✓ Check your answers!

1. True. The term "best friend" describes the type of friendship you have with your bud: a close one. That doesn't make it better than other friendships. Each friendship is valuable in its own way.

2. False. Best friends are loyal to each other—but not exclusive.

3. True. Enjoy each close friendship for what it is. You may feel close to Elizabeth because she sits next to you in youth orchestra, she understands your frustration with cello fingerings and you both love Brahms—even though you attend different schools. And you may feel close to Renee because she's in your gym class and she drops by each Saturday with the latest magazine so the two of you can try out new hairstyles—even though she doesn't know the difference between a violin and a trombone. Both Elizabeth and Renee can be your "best friends," just in different ways.

Real Girl TIPS

"I used to think that a best friend meant a perfect match. Now I know that best friends like each other enough to work things out."

Mary Ellen, age 12
Kentucky

4. True. You grow closer to some people more easily than others. Plus, you simply do not have time to make 2,756 phone calls each night!

5. False. All friends are human beings, and all human beings make mistakes. Be prepared: it is extremely likely that your best bud at some point will hurt you.* In addition, there will be a time when you hurt your best friend, even if you try not to. That's why it's important for all friends to learn to forgive—and ask for forgiveness.

*There is one Best Bud who is an exception to this rule. Read about it in Chapter 12–"Your A.B.F.F."

Best Buds Secret Code!

You and your best bud can share messages in secret when you make up your own code.

 What You Need

❋ paper

❋ pencils

❋ your best bud

What to Do

1. Choose a "code-breaker" by selecting a number from 1-26. (Example: "4")

2. Make a Code Key Chart (see the example on the next page) to create a new alphabet. In this case, the code-breaker number is 4, so the fourth letter of the alphabet, "D," replaces the first letter of the alphabet, "A." The code continues in alphabetical order. The letter "E" replaces the letter "B" in your message, and so forth, as shown below on the sample.

3. Write out words by using your code, like this:

FRIEND becomes

COFBKA

("C" replaces "F," "O" replaces "R" on so on.)

4. Name your code. The name of the sample code is "BBSC 4-4-1," which stands for "Best Buds Secret Code 4 replaces 1." That tells you that the key to breaking your code is the fourth letter of the alphabet replacing the first letter of the alphabet ("four for one").

5. Hide the key to your code in a safe place.

6. Make up a new code anytime. BBSC 16-4-1, for example, means that "P," the sixteenth letter of the alphabet, will replace "A," the first letter of the alphabet. Construct your code key chart accordingly. "BBSC 7-4-2," on the other hand, means that the first letter of the new code alphabet would be "G," which would be replaced by the second letter of the alphabet ("2" in the code), or "B."

7. Use your code with a best bud...or with yourself!

8. Decipher the message below. Use the code key chart for BBSC 4-4-1 to help you.

(Look for the answer on the bottom of this page.)

F EXSB EFAABK DLA'P TLOA FK JV EBXOQ.

_____

_____

(MPXIJ 119:11) _____

<table>
<tr><td colspan="9" align="center">**Sample Code Key Chart (BBSC 4-4-1)**</td></tr>
<tr><td>**A**</td><td>**B**</td><td>**C**</td><td>**D**</td><td>**E**</td><td>**F**</td><td>**G**</td><td>**H**</td><td>**I**</td></tr>
<tr><td>X</td><td>Y</td><td>Z</td><td>A</td><td>B</td><td>C</td><td>D</td><td>E</td><td>F</td></tr>
<tr><td>**J**</td><td>**K**</td><td>**L**</td><td>**M**</td><td>**N**</td><td>**O**</td><td>**P**</td><td>**Q**</td><td>**R**</td></tr>
<tr><td>G</td><td>H</td><td>I</td><td>J</td><td>K</td><td>L</td><td>M</td><td>N</td><td>O</td></tr>
<tr><td>**S**</td><td>**T**</td><td>**U**</td><td>**V**</td><td>**W**</td><td>**X**</td><td>**Y**</td><td>**Z**</td><td></td></tr>
<tr><td>P</td><td>Q</td><td>R</td><td>S</td><td>T</td><td>U</td><td>V</td><td>W</td><td></td></tr>
</table>

Answer: I have hidden God's word in my heart. (Psalm 119:11)

FAQs: Will We Really Be B.F.F.?
▬ ▬ ▬ ▬ ▬ ▬ ▬ (Best Friends Forever)

Forever?

Q: Holly and I are best friends. I want it to stay that way forever. Can it?

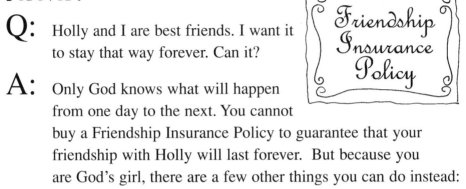

Friendship Insurance Policy

A: Only God knows what will happen from one day to the next. You cannot buy a Friendship Insurance Policy to guarantee that your friendship with Holly will last forever. But because you are God's girl, there are a few other things you can do instead:

❋ Continue to enjoy your friendship with Holly.

❋ Tell Holly often how much you appreciate her.

❋ Thank God for giving you such a good friend.

❋ Entrust your friendship with Holly to God.

God Puts It This Way

It is not for you to know the times or dates the Father has set by his own authority.
                            ~Acts 1:7

Mood Swings

Q: Kim and I are best friends, but lately she has been moody. One day she's up, the next day she's down. She says it has nothing to do with me–it's just the way she is these days. I'm not sure. Should I do anything?

A: There are several reasons why Kim's mood can change from one minute to the next:

✳ Personality. Some people have higher highs and deeper lows than others.

✳ Problems. Kim may have a problem at home or at school, and may not know how to talk about it.

✳ Adolescence. As we grow up, the chemicals in our bodies called "hormones" kick in at unexpected times. Hormones can make us laugh hysterically one minute and sob uncontrollably the next.

✳ Illness. Kim may be sick and not know it, or she may be keeping it to herself.

✳ Medication. Kim could be taking prescribed medicine for a physical condition, which may have moodiness as a side effect.

What you can do:

✳ Be accepting. Since Kim told you that you are not the problem, take her at her word.

✳ Be informed. Ask Kim, "Is there anything else bothering you?"

✳ Be helpful. If you find out that Kim is having trouble at home or at school, help her find an adult friend in whom to confide.

✳ Be supportive. Put yourself in Kim's shoes. You know how it feels to have your moods play "bouncy ball" while you're trying to get a grip!

Changes

Q: Michelle and I have been best friends for two-and-a-half years. But this year we moved up to middle school and she's hanging out with different friends. She's changing, and so am I. Help!

A: Changes! Sooner or later, everybody faces them. Right now, you and Michelle are looking smack into the face of some pretty big changes:

✳ You are meeting many new people in your new school.

✵ You are discovering new skills and interests.

✵ You are finding out your unique personality strengths and weaknesses.

✵ You are learning with what kinds of people you are most comfortable.

✵ You are making decisions about how to spend your time.

What does that mean for you?

✵ The decisions and discoveries you make will be unique to you because there is only 1 U!

✵ Those decisions and discoveries may not fit in with Michelle's.

✵ You may not feel as comfortable with Michelle as you used to feel.

✵ She may not feel as comfortable with you.

Look to **The Friendship Coach** for guidance and comfort as you go through this time of confusion. When you look to Him for help and do what He says, you can know that you're on the right track.

God Puts It This Way

We...are being transformed into his likeness with ever-increasing glory, which comes from the Lord.

~2 Corinthians 3:18

What God Means

When you rely on God to make good decisions, He will help you change in the right ways.

Talk to God

Dear God, I know I am growing up and changing, and so is (name a good friend who is changing also). Help me to lean on You to make good decisions about activities, friends and behaviors. Lead me to listen to You as I make choices. I trust You to help me change into Your likeness. In Jesus' name, Amen.

Fun Together Quiz 4-2-uv-U!

Find out how well you and your best bud know each other!

🖌 What You Need

✳ 2 sheets of paper

✳ 2 pencils

✳ quiz on page 95

✳ your best bud

What to Do

1. Give a sheet of paper to your friend. Keep one for yourself.

2. Fold your papers lengthwise in half to make two columns. The papers should remain folded until you are both completely finished with the quiz.

3. Label one column on your paper with your name and one column with your friend's name. Number both columns 1-20. Have your friend do the same.

4. Both you and your friend should start with the column that has the other person's name at the top. Both of you should answer questions 1-20 (see next page) as you think your friend would.

5. When you are done answering the questions in your friend's column, turn your paper over. This column should already be titled with your name.

6. Answer the questions for yourself. Be completely honest! Have your friend do the same on her paper.

7. When both of you are finished, open your papers. Compare the column on your paper labeled with your friend's name with her personal answers on her paper. Likewise, compare your personal answers with the column labeled with your name on her paper.

8. Each of you receives one point for each correct answer when compared with the other's personal answers. Total your scores and check your "Know-U" Ratings on the next page!

Quiz 4-2-uv-U Questions

1. Her favorite kind of pizza (brand, crust and toppings).

2. The topic of her last argument with her mom.

3. Books by her bedside right now (without looking).

4. When she grows up she'd like to be…

5. Her jeans size.

6. Number of different ways she has worn her hair this week.

7. A passage or story in the Bible she likes a lot.

8. Number of cavities she had on her last visit to the dentist.

9. The subject in school that is easiest for her.

10. Her most embarrassing moment.

11. Her favorite sport.

12. A big question she has about Jesus.

13. The subject in school that is most challenging for her.

14. City and state where she was born.

15. Where her grandparents live (both sets!).

16. Her dad's occupation.

17. How long she has lived in her present home.

18. The radio station she listens to most often.

19. Her phone number or e-mail address (extra credit if you know both!).

20. The guy she has a crush on.

After you total the number you have correct, turn
the page for your Know-U Ratings!

Know-U Ratings

16-20 points: Know-U-GR8! You know your bud! You are up-to-date on her tastes, hopes, doubts, strengths, weaknesses, schedule, family and preferences. Over time, her ideas–and yours–may change. But if you keep caring, sharing and communicating, your friendship can grow, too.

9-15 points: Know-U-well! You know a lot about your friend! Listen carefully to details she tells you–and ask what she thinks or feels–in order to know her even better. And clue her in about the specifics going on in your life, too.

8 points or less: Getting to Know-U! This is an exciting time in your friendship! You and your bud are just getting to know each other. Enjoy the discoveries you'll make as your friendship blossoms.

What's Best About Best Friends

All friends are special. But a best friend is precious because…

✳ You choose her for her–and she chooses you for you. A best friend is **valued**.

✳ You tell her things you can't tell anyone else. And she shares her secrets, too. A best friend is **close**.

✳ You know what's she going through–and she knows what you're going through. A best friend **understands** you.

✳ You spend time together, laugh together and play together. A best friend is **fun**.

❋ You let her have space–and she lets you have some, too. A best friend gives you **freedom to grow**.

❋ You won't have many in your lifetime. A best friend is **priceless**.

Make It! • Best Buds Accordion Frame

Keep photos of you and your best bud in this frame. You can even change the pictures from time to time.

What You Need

❋ two pieces poster board, 14" x 4½"

❋ acid-free scrapbooking glue

❋ paint pens or markers

❋ stickers

❋ scissors

❋ ruler

❋ pencil

❋ photos

What to Do

1. With a ruler and pencil, measure and lightly mark off each piece of poster board into four 3½" sections. Use the tip of a scissors blade to score along pencil lines on both pieces of poster board. Fold along the scored markings.

2. Choose one piece of poster board to use as the front of the accordion frame. Mark and cut out a 2" x 2½" rectangle on each of the four sections.

3. With acid-free scrapbooking glue, attach the front of the accordion frame to the back along the side edges, bottom edge and scored folds. Leave the top edges unglued to insert photos. Trim the corners into curves.

4. Use paint pens or markers to decorate the accordion frame with dots, dashes and scallops, resembling the running lights on a theatre marquis. If desired, add stickers. Allow the frame to dry completely.

5. Insert photos into the frame.

6. Display your **Best Buds Accordion Frame** on a table or desk, or give it to your best bud!

Did You Know?

Two Bible characters who had an especially close friendship were David and Jonathan. They had a secret code: Jonathan used special objects to warn David and save his life. What were these special objects? The answer is on page 185.

Chapter Seven

One of the Girls

"Accept one another, then, just as Christ accepted you."

~Romans 15:7

✳ What Every Girl Needs to ✳ Know About Popularity

Myth Kids in The Popular Group are elite.

Truth Kids in The Popular Group are a lot like other kids.

- ✳ They worry about how they look when they get dressed in the morning, just like you worry.
- ✳ They are afraid others won't like them, just like you fear.
- ✳ They want to be accepted and liked for who they really are, just like you do.

Myth Kids in The Popular Group have more friends than anyone else.

Truth Popular means "well-liked."

Kids in The Popular Group may not necessarily have more friends than anyone else (in fact, some people don't even like them). What they do have, however, is an image. But the truly popular person is someone who is genuinely liked by many different people. She values people for who they are on the inside. And they treasure her in return.

Myth Lots of girls think that popularity is a matter of chance. To be popular, they must…

- ✳ Be born that way, or sprinkled with special popularity dust at birth.
- ✳ Receive the approval of a Popular Group member, and then be accepted as one of them.
- ✳ Be resigned to a life of unpopularity.

Truth You create your own popularity. Be a true friend to enough people, and you will suddenly find out one day that you are popular!

QUIZ! One of the Girls

How do you try to fit in with the crowd? For each question, circle the answer that best describes you. Then turn the page to check your answers!

1. Your science class takes a field trip to a waterfront marina to study how oysters are harvested. You…

A. Immediately volunteer to operate the rake and pull oysters out of the bay, even though girls in your group shriek, "That is so disgusting!"

B. Notice your friends moving toward the sorting bin. You hurry to join them. You want to see and feel what the oysters are like.

C. Hang back when one of your friends says, "There is no way I will ever touch those slimy things!"–although you are secretly curious.

2. A new girl moves into the neighborhood. You…

A. Go over to her house and introduce yourself while the moving van is still in the driveway: "Would you like to walk with me to the bus stop tomorrow?"

B. Worry that if she doesn't fit in after you make friends with her, it will reflect badly on you. You wait to meet her at school.

C. Completely ignore her.

3. Your mom volunteers to chaperone the youth orchestra trip. You…

A. Think it is fine. She'll bring along extra snacks for you and your friends.

B. Make her promise to pretend she doesn't know you.

C. Beg her not to go. She doesn't speak English well. It would be so embarrassing!

101

4. It's Career Day at school, and you learn that Joellen's mom is an attorney and Claire's stepfather started a pet store chain that now has 23 locations. Hardly anyone has signed up to attend those two presentations. You…

A. Go to both presentations anyway, since you are interested in becoming an animal-rights advocate.

B. Are overwhelmed by indecision until Claire says, "Didn't you tell me you want to be a vet? Come talk with my stepfather!"

C. Pretend you are interested in fashion merchandising like 97 percent of the other girls, and squeeze into the last seat available at that presentation.

5. Colleen wrote a letter to the editor that was just printed in the school newsletter. You…

A. See Colleen in the hallway, walk up to her and say, "Great letter, Colleen. I agree that a girl's table tennis team is a good idea."

B. Wait to see how your friends react to Colleen's letter before you speak to her about it.

C. Overhear three football players teasing Colleen about the letter, and decide to act like you never read it.

✔ Check your answers!

If you checked **mostly A's**, you are an **Individualist**! Congratulations, you think for yourself. You choose to act on your beliefs and interests, rather than waiting for approval from your peers. You are unwilling to give up who you are in order to be one of the girls. Keep it up!

If you checked **mostly B's**, you are a **Fence Sitter**! You feel uncomfortable deciding what to do until you see what others think. Be careful. If you always go along with the crowd, then eventually you will lose your individuality.

If you checked **mostly C's**, you are like a **Chameleon**. You know, that creature whose skin color changes to match its surroundings? You make decisions based on what everyone else thinks instead of what you want to do or think. Don't be so eager to be one of the girls that you lose sight of who God made you to be. Think for yourself and act like yourself, not someone else.

 ## God Puts It This Way

Do not follow the crowd in doing wrong.

~Exodus 23:2

 ## Write About It

Make a list of times when it was hard for you to think for yourself.

_____

_____

_____

 ## Talk to God

Dear God, it's hard for me to think for myself because I want to fit in with the girls. In particular, it was hard when (read the list you made above). Strengthen me. Give me insight to know when I am about to go along with the crowd rather than listening to You and being myself. I want to be Your girl. In Jesus' name, Amen.

Did You Know?

Two "popular" groups in Jerusalem during Jesus' time were the Pharisees, a religious and political party, and the Sadducees, a group of wealthy Jewish scholars and leaders. Which group was Jesus in? See page 185.

6 True Rules About Being Cool

Rule 1 ~ Everybody likes to feel they are cool.

Rule 2 ~ There is something cool about everyone.

Rule 3 ~ Some people appoint themselves judges of cool, when they really aren't.

Rule 4 ~ **The Friendship Coach** is the cool rule originator. He says what's cool and what's not cool.

Rule 5 ~ **The Friendship Coach** knows all the cool things about you that others may miss.

Rule 6 ~ **The Friendship Coach** finds cool things in everybody.

HEY, I'VE NEVER SEEN THAT COLOR OF NAIL POLISH BEFORE, BUT I THINK IT'S COOL!

👉 Try This

Be cool! Follow **The Friendship Coach's** lead. Find things about people that that you think are cool. Then tell them! But beware: you're going to make lots of friends this way. People like being accepted rather than judged. Pretty soon, you will have a long line of friends who have noticed that you notice their coolness!

God Puts It This Way

For in the same way you judge others, you will be judged, and with the measure you use, it will be measured to you.

~Matthew 7:2

 **When There's a New Girl**

Mark the box you think is best.

1. You walk into band rehearsal on Thursday afternoon and there's a new girl sitting in your chair. "Hey, that's my seat!" you whine loudly. "Why are you sitting here?"

☐ Do this   ☐ Do something different

2. "Have you talked with that new girl from Tennessee yet?" you whisper to Carlie. "She has the weirdest accent."

☐ Do this   ☐ Do something different

3. "I realize that you only moved here three weeks ago and we're just getting to know each other," you say to Arianna, a new girl. "But I'd like to invite you to my swim party."

☐ Do this   ☐ Do something different

4. "It's so much better here than in Awaysville" you point out to Morgan, a new girl. "Aren't you happy you moved here?"

☐ Do this   ☐ Do something different

5. "I'm so glad you and your family are coming to our church," you say to Shari, a new girl. "It's great to have another girl in the youth group!"

☐ Do this   ☐ Do something different

✔ **Check your answers!**

1. **Do something different!** New girls want to fit in, not feel like an intrusion. Don't be territorial. Try asking, "How long have you been playing the clarinet?"

2. **Do something different!** A new girl already feels as if she sticks out. She will only feel worse when you point out differences in her looks, manners or speech. Instead of making fun of her, you can help her feel accepted by complimenting her French braids or her sense of humor.

3. **Do this!** Nothing can make a new girl feel more welcome than to be invited to a party. By reaching out to Arianna, you show that you care about her feelings. Plus, you're giving her the opportunity to make new friends at the party.

4. **Do something different!** Telling Morgan that her new community is better than the one she left puts her in an awkward position. She may like it here, but she may not feel at home just yet. And if she is still homesick for Awaysville, she may agree with you aloud, but only to avoid offending you.

5. **Do this!** It can put a new girl at ease to know that she is fulfilling a need. You've made Shari feel wanted, important and part of the group.

So what are you to do when there's a new girl?

✳ Remember the time you were in her shoes and you were the new girl. Maybe it was when you entered a different school. Or joined a softball team when you'd never held a bat before.

✳ Remember the uncertainty and nervousness you felt.

✳ You know what to do: Make her feel welcome and accepted.

God Puts It This Way

When did we see you a stranger and invite you in…The King will reply, "I tell you the truth, whatever you did for one of the least of these brothers of mine, you did for me."

~Matthew 25:38, 40

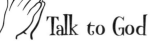

Talk to God

Dear God, show me how to treat the new girls You put into my life, such as (name a new girl). Help me to consider her feelings, make her feel welcome and let her know that I accept her. In Jesus' name, Amen.

FAQs: But She's So Different

In this edition of FAQs, God's girls get some answers from each other!

Divorce

Q: My friend Ginny's parents are getting a divorce. I've never been in that situation and I don't know what to do. How should I be her friend?

A: "Listen to Ginny. Let her know you care. You can't take away how hurt she is, but you can be supportive."

~Darlene, age 10, New York

A Different Kind of Family

Q: My new friend, Latrisha, lives with her aunt. She only sees her mom once a year and she has never met her dad. I feel awkward inviting her over to my house because I live with my mom, dad, sister and two brothers, and I don't want her to feel uncomfortable. What should I do?

A: "I live with my grandmother and I was in Latrisha's situation when I met my friend Nora. Nora invited me to her house for dinner one night, and her family made me feel like I was one of them. I loved the noise, teasing and bantering. But the best thing Nora did was come to my house when I invited her. That's when I knew that she accepted me and was a real friend. Now, Nora and I spend so much time together that my grandmother calls her 'my other granddaughter'! She even asks Nora what to get me for Christmas and my birthday."

~Shereece, age 12, Texas

Money

Q: My friend Marcia has a terrific sense of humor. She and I have always had so much fun together. But she never let on how well off her parents are. One day I went to her house–and I saw that it is beautiful. Now, I'm intimidated. Why would Marcia want to be my friend?

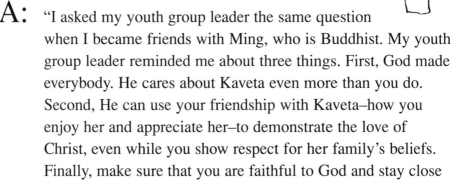

A: "The friends that matter the most to me are the ones who like me because of who I am on the inside–not just because my parents are both lawyers and make good salaries. I'm comfortable with these friends because they are real. Everyone is a person no matter what is in her wallet."

~Thea, age 11, Virginia

God Puts It This Way

Rich and poor have this in common: The Lord is the Maker of them all.

~Proverbs 22:2

Another Religion

Q: My friend Kaveta is Hindu. She is really smart, and she helps me in math class. Is it okay to have a friend who is not a Christian?

A: "I asked my youth group leader the same question when I became friends with Ming, who is Buddhist. My youth group leader reminded me about three things. First, God made everybody. He cares about Kaveta even more than you do. Second, He can use your friendship with Kaveta–how you enjoy her and appreciate her–to demonstrate the love of Christ, even while you show respect for her family's beliefs. Finally, make sure that you are faithful to God and stay close

to Him while you are friends with Kaveta. Ask another
Christian girl or adult friend to pray with you for her!"

~Natalie, age 13, California

 ## God Puts It This Way

*In [Jesus] and through faith in him we may approach
God with freedom and confidence.*

~Ephesians 3:12

 ## Talk to God

Dear God, my friend (name your friend) has a different home life
from me in this way (describe the difference). Show me how to find
ways to be friends with everybody in spite of our differences. I want
to be that kind of friend. Show me how when I see (name your friend)
today. In Jesus' name, Amen.

Make It! • **Truly Cool Sleeve Clips**

These clasps keep you cool: they convert short-
sleeve T-shirts into sleeveless tops when the weather is hot! Plus, they
remind you that Jesus is the One who is really cool.

 ## What You Need

❋ ribbon, 1" wide

❋ Velcro, 1" wide

❋ fabric paint

❋ fabric glue

❋ ruler

❋ scissors

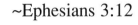

What to Do

1. Measure and cut two pieces of ribbon, each 8 inches long. Lay the ribbons flat on your work surface. Turn under and glue ½" of one raw end of each ribbon. Flip the ribbons over. Turn under and glue ½" of the other raw end of each ribbon to the opposite side of the first. For each ribbon, you should now have one raw end turned and glued to one side, and the other raw end turned and glued to the opposite side.

2. Measure and cut two strips of Velcro at 1¼" long, one strip for each sleeve clip. Separate the strips.

3. Lay the ribbons flat on your work surface, one glued raw edge of each ribbon facing up. Glue one piece from each separated Velcro strip over the top of each glued raw edge, making sure the Velcro lines up with the glued ribbon edge. Flip the ribbons over. Repeat the procedure for the opposite side.

> ### Did You Know?
>
> Jesus had a close group of friends. There were 12 of them. What were they called? Check your answer on page 185.

4. Allow the sleeve clips to dry completely.

5. With fabric glue, write the words "true cool" on each sleeve clip, making the "t" in "true" as a cross. Decorate the end of the clip with a fabric paint cross.

6. Allow the paint to dry completely.

7. Clip up your T-shirt sleeves with your **Truly Cool Sleeve Clips!**

Chapter Eight

Friendship 9-1-1

"Call to me and I will answer you."

~Jeremiah 33:3

Friendship emergency tip revealed

By Bud D. Forlyfe
ASSOCIATES PRESS

SAN FRIENDCISCO, PALIFORNIA – Today at the Friendship All-Star Games, God's girls revealed a guaranteed winners' strategy for friendship emergencies: consult the Friendship Coach.

"Every All-Star God's girl I interviewed uses this strategy," said Associates Press reporter Ima Friend. "Each one told me that she got to be a winner in the Friendship Game by consulting the Friendship Coach."

When pressed, God's girls explained further. "Sometimes I feel more confused or upset than usual, and I know I need extra help," said Keisha R., 11, of Lansing, Mich. "In the Friendship Game, it's easy to get distracted by conflicting advice from other people–even my closest friends. That's when I am sure to talk with the Friendship Coach."

Claudia B., 12, of Kingsport, Tenn., described the tactic as like dialing a heavenly 9-1-1. "No matter what my friendship emergency, I just call out to the Coach," she said. "He always answers."

Several of God's girls pointed out the Friendship Coach's personal phone number (see box below) as a key part of this successful approach.

God's girls say the most frequent friendship emergencies are jealousy, gossip, teasing, rejection, betrayal and being stuck in the middle. "Anytime I face one of these," said Juanita J., 13, of Tucson, Ariz., "I know it's time to call on the Friendship Coach."

> ### The Friendship Coach's Phone Number: Jeremiah 33:3

Spotlight on...

The Green-Eyed Monster

Shine that spotlight into the closet of your heart...that's where The Green-Eyed Monster hides out! Find out how to uncloak that nasty brute and kick It out of your life.

Also known as: Jealousy

Sometimes called: Envy, Covetousness

First Sighting: In the Garden of Eden. Adam and Eve encountered the Monster (appearing as Covetousness) when they wanted knowledge that wasn't theirs.

Fame and Notoriety: The Green-Eyed Monster later came into the spotlight on a mountaintop in the desert of Sinai, where It was identified for the Israelites in the Ten Commandments:

> *You shall not covet your neighbor's house. You shall not covet your neighbor's wife, or his manservant or maidservant, his ox or donkey, or anything that belongs to your neighbor.*
>
> ~Exodus 20:17

The Monster's real problem: Ingratitude. The Monster–jealousy–can never be satisfied. It always wants more of what It already has, or It wants what someone else has.

Who the Monster attacks: Anyone. Everyone. All members of the human race.

Where the Monster works: The Green-Eyed Monster works both within individual girls and between friends. Participants in a God's girls survey reported encounters with the Monster over physical appearance, boys, other girlfriends, clothes, achievements, possessions, grades, homes, families, schools, abilities–and countless other issues. All of the survey participants agreed that where jealousy is, "you find disorder and every evil practice." (James 3:16)

What happens during a Monster attack:

1. You notice something good that someone else has or is.

2. You compare yourself or your possessions with the other person's—and find yourself lacking.

3. You begin to turn green with jealousy (note: shade of green may vary from girl to girl!).

To chase the Monster away:

1. Recognize the Monster when It appears in one of three forms: jealousy, envy or covetousness.

2. Resist attempts at comparison and competition, two of the Monster's favorite tools.

3. Give praise and appreciation to **The Friendship Coach.** The Monster disappears when there is genuine gratitude.

Builders and Bulldozers

Some words encourage people. Some words tear people down. You can learn to be a builder with your words rather than a bulldozer. Label with a "**+**" the expressions that build up others and write a "**—**" next to those that bulldoze and destroy.

_____ 1. In your face, loser.

_____ 2. Awesome…way to go!

_____ 3. You blew it.

_____ 4. Great job.

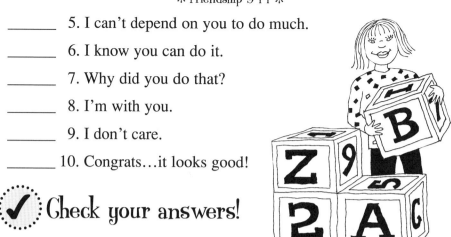

_____ 5. I can't depend on you to do much.

_____ 6. I know you can do it.

_____ 7. Why did you do that?

_____ 8. I'm with you.

_____ 9. I don't care.

_____ 10. Congrats…it looks good!

 Check your answers!

Odd numbers: The Bulldozers (-)

These words tear down rather than build up. You may use them in frustration or without thinking, not realizing their power to bulldoze through another person's heart. These kinds of expressions are destructive.

Even numbers: The Builders (+)

These words build up rather than tear down. When you use them, you have other people's needs in mind (rather than your own). These kinds of expressions strengthen other people.

 God Puts It This Way

Do not let any unwholesome talk come out of your mouths, but only what is helpful for building others up according to their needs, that it may benefit those who listen.

~Ephesians 4:29

Write About It

Write below some "Builders" and "Bulldozers" you used or heard someone else use today.

_____

_____

_____

Bickering, Gossip, Lies and Teasing

These words hurt more than others. Now you can know why.

Bickering

Also known as: quarreling, arguing, interfering, fighting

What happens: You disagree with one or more friends, then everyone gets involved. Someone always gets hurt.

Damage potential: High. Similar to a flood!

 ### God Puts It This Way

Starting a quarrel is like breaching a dam.

~Proverbs 17:14

Gossip

Also known as: spreading rumors

What happens: You hear a juicy tidbit about one of your friends. You share it with "only" one or two others. They also share it with "only" one or two others. And so on. Soon, dozens of people know the tidbit that your friend wanted to keep private–and she gets hurt.

Damage potential: High. Resembles a fire out of control!

 ### God Puts It This Way

Consider what a great forest is set on fire by a small spark.

~James 3:5

Lies

Also known as: deceit, telling untruths, portraying a falsehood

What happens: You say something to a friend that is not exactly, completely the truth–or it is a full-fledged untruth. Lies are told to either protect yourself or hurt someone else.

Damage potential: Very High. Akin to crushing and destroying!

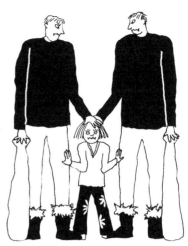

 ## God Puts It This Way
A deceitful tongue crushes the spirit.

~Proverbs 15:4

Teasing

Also known as: kidding, taunting, mocking

What happens: You make fun of a friend. You may say you are "only joking," or you may be provoking her on purpose. Either way, she ends up getting hurt.

Damage potential: High. Much like using a knife to injure and cut!

 ## God Puts It This Way
Reckless words pierce like a sword.

~Proverbs 12:18

 ## Talk to God

Dear God, I don't want my words to hurt others. But today, it happened when I (name a situation). I am sorry for using these words in a damaging way. Please forgive me, and help me not to do it again. In Jesus' name, Amen.

● Make It! ● Builder's Bookmark

This bookmark can remind you to use words that "build up" other people. You can also make a **Builder's Bookmark** for a friend to show her that you think she is "fantastic, above and beyond, and simply spectacular"!

 ## What You Need

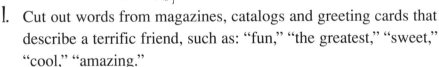

* ✳ 8" x 1¾" poster board
* ✳ magazines, catalogs or used greeting cards
* ✳ clear packaging tape, 2" wide
* ✳ acid-free scrapbooking glue
* ✳ scissors
* ✳ strand of yarn, 20" long
* ✳ hole punch

What to Do

1. Cut out words from magazines, catalogs and greeting cards that describe a terrific friend, such as: "fun," "the greatest," "sweet," "cool," "amazing."

2. Use the poster board as your bookmark's base. Arrange the cut-out words on one side of the bookmark base, as in a collage. Attach them with acid-free scrapbooking glue. Trim the edges. Repeat this procedure for the opposite side of the bookmark.

3. Allow the bookmark to dry completely.

4. Cut two pieces of clear packaging tape to cover each side of the bookmark. Attach the tape to the bookmark. Smooth out any wrinkles. Trim the edges.

5. Use the hole punch to punch a hole at the end of bookmark.

6. Fold the strand of yarn lengthwise so that it is doubled and 10" long. Knot together the two loose ends to form a tail.

7. Thread 1" of the folded end through the bookmark hole. Slightly open up the folded end so it becomes a loop. Slip the knotted end through the loop and pull the yarn all the way through to create a bookmark tail.

8. Place your bookmark in the book you are reading now, or give it to a friend and tell her she is "fantastic"!

Hint: Words in magazines, catalogs and greeting cards are printed in all kinds of fonts and colors. Select different sizes and shapes to give variety to your bookmark collage. Small words are particularly useful for filling in gaps.

Real Girl TIPS

"One time, I got an A+ on a book report. My friend Nicki got a B-. She said, 'Great job! I loved your report!' That made me feel fantastic."

Allison, age 10
Maryland

I GOT R-E-J-E-C-T-E-D

What you can do when it happens to you.

R **REMEMBER** who you are: God's girl! Others are not always right about you, but God always is.

E **EXAMINE** your feelings. Envy, bitterness, frustration and resentment are your real enemies when you've been hurt, not other people.

J **JESUS** knows how you feel. He was rejected–a lot. Many people didn't like Him while He lived on earth, and still don't today, because He is different from them.

E **EXPECT** your emotions to take time to heal. And **EXPECT** that God will help you grow from this experience!

G **CALL** on the Coach! Tell God how you feel. Be completely honest. Ask Him to help you.

T **TALK** about it with someone you trust. Tell a parent, teacher or adult friend what happened.

E **EVALUATE** how you can help another friend when she is rejected and hurting. Use your experience to encourage someone else.

D **DON'T** give up. **DO** try again.

Spotlight on...

The Third Wheel

The Third Wheel doesn't want center stage. She already feels singled out–and left out. But this spotlight can give her some ideas about what to do next.

Also known as:
the odd girl out

Recognized in this phrase: "Two's company, three's a crowd."

Situation she finds herself in: The Friendship Triangle. Two of her friends are already close to each other–and growing closer. She is beginning to wonder if she fits in.

Kinds of Friendship Triangles

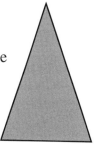

The Acute Triangle. Two friends have gotten so close that they consider the third one, known as "The Third Wheel," to be a nuisance.

The Obtuse Triangle. Two friends do not have a clue that The Third Wheel feels excluded.

The Equilateral Triangle. The preferable Friendship Triangle. All three friends recognize that a three-way friendship can be special. And they treat it that way.

Steps The Third Wheel can take that are NOT recommended:

✳ Pout

✳ Whine

✳ Complain

✳ Pit one friend against the other in the hopes of getting one of them to "be her best friend."

Steps The Third Wheel can take that ARE recommended:

✳ Recognize that all friendships are different.

✳ Tell the other two friends that she feels excluded. They may have no idea!

✳ Find out if she has offended either friend in any way.

✳ Ask her friends if they need more privacy–and if so, give it to them.

✳ Consider investing some time and energy in other friendships.

Talk to God

Dear God, I feel left out. It feels lonely. Show me today someone else who also feels left out. Let me be a good friend to her. And keep me from making someone else feel like The Third Wheel when we are together. In Jesus' name, Amen.

FAQs: Betrayed!

Expectations

Q: Our math teacher told Annie and me, "Stop chatting so much, girls, for the last time." When we didn't, she made us stay inside during recess. But the worst of it was this: my friend Christine didn't take my side! Christine says that I was just as much to blame for losing recess as Annie. Christine betrayed me, didn't she?

A: Ask yourself this question (answer honestly!): Was Annie 100%, completely and thoroughly, without any smidgen of doubt, no question marks involved, the only one at fault during the incident in math class? It is unfair to call Christine a traitor when she simply tells you the facts.

Bottom line: Don't confuse betrayal with unrealistic expectations you have for your friend.

Motivations

Q: A group of girls in the school chorus don't like Mr. Bartlett, the chorus director. They hid the chorus books in the back of the kindergarten closet the day before the concert. I went to him by myself, told him where to find the books and asked him to keep our conversation a secret. Mr. Bartlett kept my secret. The girls never found out who told him. Did I betray my friends?

A: No. At the heart of betrayal are hurtful motivations. You revealed your helpful motivations by:

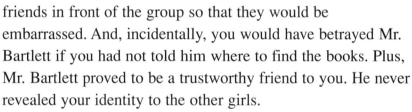

1. Sharing what you knew. This helped Mr. Bartlett and the chorus to go forward with the concert.

2. Asking to remain anonymous. You would have shown hurtful motivations if you had tattled on your friends in front of the group so that they would be embarrassed. And, incidentally, you would have betrayed Mr. Bartlett if you had not told him where to find the books. Plus, Mr. Bartlett proved to be a trustworthy friend to you. He never revealed your identity to the other girls.

Bottom line: Always check your motivations. Do the right thing for the right reason.

Jumping to Conclusions

Q: I just found out that I have dyslexia, a learning disability. I told only one person: my friend Rena. She promised she wouldn't tell anyone. Now, Kenneth and Michael want to know why I'll be moved to a different reading group. I think Rena betrayed me. What should I do?

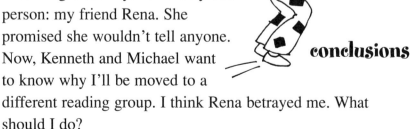

conclusions

A: Be careful not to jump to conclusions because…

1. It is possible that Rena kept your secret. Kenneth and

Michael may have heard about changes in the classroom setup, and not know anything else.

2. You should ask Rena if she passed along your secret. Then you will know the truth firsthand. If she is a real friend, she will either apologize for betraying a confidence, or understand your sensitive feelings even though she revealed nothing.

3. Rena will appreciate the fact that you came to her first, rather than jumping to conclusions.

Bottom line: Don't jump to conclusions and assume betrayal. Get the facts!

God Puts It This Way

If your brother sins against you, go and show him his fault, just between the two of you. If he listens to you, you have won your brother over.

~Matthew 18:15

Talk to God

Dear God, I feel betrayed by my friend (name the friend and the situation). Do I have unrealistic expectations? Show me if I am jumping to conclusions. Give me the courage to go to my friend and talk with her. I want to be a good friend in the right way. In Jesus' name, Amen.

Help! I'm Stuck in the Middle!

Rosa and Elyse are at it again…arguing with each other. It's frustrating, annoying and nerve-wracking—and you feel pulled in opposite directions. Take heart. You can do what seems impossible: be friends  with both of them while they work out their differences.

What You Can Do

DO be an observer, not a participant. Let the other two girls duke it out!

DO talk about other things. Crack a joke to relieve the tension.

DO be available to listen. You are still friends, even if they are enemies.

DO give them time. Their disagreement may not get resolved by the end of history class.

DO pray for Rosa and Elyse. Ask **The Friendship Coach** to show them how to reconcile.

DO talk about it privately with an older girl or adult you trust.

What You DON'T Want to Do

DON'T ignore one of them–or both. Friends stay friends, even when times are hard.

DON'T be a messenger. Tell Rosa and Elyse to communicate directly with each other.

DON'T take sides. When Rosa and Elyse make up, you will want to be able to enjoy your threesome again.

DON'T gossip about their argument. It will only compound the problem.

DON'T try to "fix it." This is their fight, not yours.

Afterward...

DON'T bring up their fight.

DO think about what you learned from being stuck in the middle (see "Write about it" on the next page).

DO have fun with your friends!

Write About It

On another sheet of paper, make two lists: "What I did when I was stuck in the middle" and "What I didn't do when I was stuck in the middle." Which items from each list worked best? Highlight those with a yellow marker.

♪ A Note to Myself

Today's date: _____

Mark this page in a special way. Return to it the next time you are stuck in the middle between two friends.

FAQs: When Not to Be a Friend

Worn Out

Q: I know that **The Secret of Friendship** is to be a good friend because everyone wants one and no one can ever have too many. I have taken that to heart, maybe too much. I've spent so much time being a good friend to people that I feel worn out. Is it time for me not to be a friend?

A: There's one friendship you have neglected, believe it or not. You have forgotten to be friends with you. God wants you to "love your neighbor as yourself" (James 2:8). So try to keep a balance: be a good friend to others and be a good friend to yourself.

Wearing Down

Q: I have a really close friend who is trying to get me to do something I know for sure would get me in tons of trouble with my parents. When I say no, she calls me a wimp and says no one will ever find out. I'm getting tired of saying no and am really tempted to go along with her, just to get her off my back. But I know what she wants to do is wrong. Is it time for me not to be a friend? P.S. She says I'm her only friend.

A: Saying you are someone's friend is altogether different from acting like a friend. This person is not being a true friend when she tries repeatedly to get you to do something wrong. It's time for you to be her friend in a different way:

1. Follow your good instincts. Don't get into trouble just because of one person. Tell your friend that you can't spend time with her anymore.

2. Encourage your friend to talk to an adult about her problems.

3. Go to a teacher, youth group worker, school counselor or adult friend. Tell that person about your problem with your friend and ask for his or her support. You will need it! This girl may keep teasing you and needling you even after you say no one final time.

Wasting My Time?

Q: I have been trying to be friends with Suzanne, a girl at school. But she makes fun of me because I go to church. She says that I'm a nerd because I don't cuss, that I'm a teacher's pet because I try to be polite, and that I'm a loser because I'm nice to some of the quiet kids in the class. Is it time for me not to be a friend to her?

A: Your first step is to make sure you are on the right track. Ask yourself these questions (answer honestly!):

1. Do you make fun of Suzanne because she doesn't go to church? (If so, that's not a good move. You're treating her the exact same way she is treating you.)

2. Do you lecture Suzanne about her behavior? (If so, that's not a good move. You're not her mom!)

3. Do you brag to Suzanne about the way you treat others? (If so, that's not a good move. Braggarts don't make very good friends.)

If you honestly answered no to these questions, congratulations! Other people have noticed that you are following the number one rule of all: you are putting God first in your life!

> ### Did You Know?
>
> Jesus was betrayed by one of His closest friends. What was his name? Check your answer on page 185.

God Puts It This Way

"Love the Lord your God with all your heart and with all your soul and with all your mind." This is the first and greatest commandment.

~Matthew 22:37-38

Talk to God

Dear God, sometimes it's hard to know when to be a friend in a different way. Right now, I'm not sure what to do about (name a friendship that confuses you, and why it's confusing). Show me what to do about this friendship. Give me the strength to do what is right. In Jesus' name, Amen.

● Make It! ● Sweet Words Lip Gloss

Now you can watch your words in a delightful, pleasing way!

 ## What You Need

✳ solid vegetable shortening

✳ honey

✳ powdered unsweetened drink mix

✳ very hot water

✳ measuring spoons

✳ bowls

✳ spoon

✳ lip gloss pot

✳ paint pens or fabric paints

✳ glitter glue

✳ craft glue

✳ small rhinestones or sequins

What to Do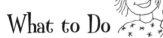

1. To make lip gloss, combine one tablespoon of solid vegetable shortening and one teaspoon of honey in a bowl. In a different bowl, measure ¼ teaspoon of drink mix. Add a few drops of very hot water until the drink mix crystals dissolve. Add the drink mixture to the shortening and honey mixture and blend thoroughly.

2. With paint pens or fabric paints, write "Sweet Words Lip Gloss" around the outside of the lip gloss pot. Decorate the top of the pot with glitter glue, small rhinestones and sequins as you want. Allow the lip gloss pot to dry completely.

3. Carefully fill the pot with lip gloss.

4. Apply your **Sweet Words Lip Gloss** to your lips!

Hint: You can darken the lip gloss shade by using more drink mix. Lip gloss will keep several weeks in an airtight pot without spoiling.

 ## God Puts It This Way

Pleasant words are a honeycomb, sweet to the soul and healing to the bones.

~Proverbs 16:24

Chapter Nine

Working It Out

"As far as it depends on you, live
at peace with everyone."

~Romans 12:18

✳ What You Gotta Know to Fight Fair ✳

Here is how God's girl can do her part.

1 ## Keep it private.

Your disagreement is with one person. The entire school does not need to get involved.

2 ## Talk it out.

✳ Find a time when you and your friend can talk without interruption.

✳ Tell your friend what bothers you, and why.

✳ Listen to her side of the story.

3 ## Take responsibility for your part.

✳ If you were wrong, say so.

✳ Some words don't work if you are trying to fight fair.

"It's not my fault!"

"Don't blame me!"

4 ## Be willing to say, "I'm sorry."

5 ## Be willing to say, "I forgive you."

6 ## Keep trying!

God Puts It This Way

As far as it depends on you, live at peace with everyone.

~Romans 12:18

What God Means

You can't be responsible for everyone else's part in a disagreement. But you should do your part to get along.

Talk to God

Dear God, I'm not getting along with (name a friend and your conflict). Help me take responsibility for my part. Help me apologize to my friend. I am counting on You to show me how. In Jesus' name, Amen.

QUIZ! Do You Own This Problem?

When a problem belongs to someone else, you must leave it alone or you will be meddling. But sometimes you own the problem, and you must face it. That's called responsibility. It can be hard to know the difference. Find out if you own these problems.

1. "You need to catch up with your homework in this class, Teresa," says Mrs. Sperling, the math teacher, to your friend. "I'm concerned that you haven't turned in anything all week long." Mrs. Sperling walks away. Teresa looks at you and rolls her eyes.

You Own This Problem   You Don't Own This Problem

2. "But it's not my fault!" you whine to your mom when she asks why your room is a mess. "Bonnie was here all afternoon, and she didn't help me clean up before she went home."

You Own This Problem   You Don't Own This Problem

3. Julia got mad at you today. You were really impolite to her when you told her that her sweater didn't look very good with her jeans. Then all the other girls started making fun of her.

You Own This Problem   You Don't Own This Problem

4. You cracked a joke about taking showers after gym class. All the other girls started laughing. Ms. Greystone made you stay after class. *She needs to loosen up,* you think.

You Own This Problem   You Don't Own This Problem

5. Kelly, your best bud, called you on the phone after she was supposed to be in bed. Her parents took away her phone privileges for a week.

You Own This Problem   You Don't Own This Problem

6. You overhear Cassie say to Lynn, "I heard that Val isn't Kara's friend anymore."

You Own This Problem   You Don't Own This Problem

✓ Check your answers!

1. You don't own this problem! Teresa is responsible for her own homework, and you are responsible for yours. But you could offer to study with her.
2. You own this problem! Your mom made it clear that keeping your room neat is your job–regardless of who helps you mess it up. Next time, ask Bonnie to help you pick up things before she leaves.

3. You own this problem! You need to apologize to Julia. Not only were your comments insensitive, but you also shared them with her while other people were around–and ended up embarrassing her in the process.

4. You own this problem! Ms. Greystone is not to blame for enforcing rules that you may not like. Respect her authority.

5. You don't own this problem! Kelly picked up the phone and dialed against her parents' wishes. She is responsible for her own behavior. Just be sure you aren't encouraging her to go against her parents' rules.

6. You don't own this problem! Val and Kara can work out their differences without interference from you. Besides, neither one told you directly that they were having a fight. Instead, you overheard it from a third party. Don't meddle!

What to Say When You're Hurting

The wrong words can fuel a fight. Choose a different way to say how you feel and turn away the tide of hurt.

Instead of saying...

> *Leave me alone.*
> *Go away.*

We use these words to protect ourselves from more hurt. But these words can backfire, and provoke a friend to quarrel louder and longer.

Try saying...

> *Could we please talk later?*
> *I don't feel like talking right now.*
> *I need some time by myself.*

These words give you time to think about your hurt feelings, rather than arguing while you are upset.

Instead of saying...

Shut up!

We use this expression to stop another person's hurtful talk. But these two little words are very nasty themselves. When we use them, we end up hurting others in the same way we've just been hurt.

Try saying...

I need a break from talking with you right now.

I don't like it when you talk like that. Please stop.

This is annoying. Stop now, please.

These words allow you to share your hurt feelings without being rude. They also can put a stop to annoying jabber.

Instead of saying...

You're not my friend anymore.

I hate you.

We use these expressions when we are frustrated with a friend and see no way out. But these words are like a cruel knife. They are very damaging.

Try saying...

You upset me when you...

You hurt me when you...

These words do two things at once: they show a friend how you feel, and they point to the specific behavior that hurt you. These words are constructive rather than destructive.

Real Girl TIPS

"I didn't want to forgive Tracie. But I kept feeling bad. Once I decided I didn't want to feel that way anymore, I talked to her and was able to forgive."

Denise, age 12
Ohio

God Puts It This Way

A gentle answer turns away wrath, but a harsh word stirs up anger.

~Proverbs 15:1

What God Means

Angry words make a fight worse. Say what you feel in a gentler way and you will have a better outcome.

Talk to God

Dear God, when I am hurt, I use angry words. Remind me the next time to try some new expressions. I want to be able to work things out with my friends. In Jesus' name, Amen.

Write About It

When was the last time you used one of the angry expressions? Write about it. Then write about it again, this time substituting one of the new sets of words. Practice saying your new words so you'll be ready next time!

_____

_____

_____

_____

_____

_____

The Secret to Revenge

A friend has just hurt you badly and you want revenge. What is **The Secret to Revenge**? Check your answer below.

- ☐ 1. Get revenge by yourself–and quickly. Dish the hurt right back to her.

- ☐ 2. Wait awhile. Soon she'll be hurt be someone else, and you can gloat.

- ☐ 3. Moan, fuss, fret, whine and feel sorry for yourself.

- ☐ 4. Be nice to her in return.

Check your answers!

If you checked...

1. Get revenge by yourself–and quickly. Dish the hurt right back to her.

Consider This

It is God's right, not yours, to take care of wrongs. Plus, He is much better at it than you ever could be. Don't try to steal the job away from Him!

God Puts It This Way

Do not take revenge, my friends, but leave room for God's wrath, for it is written: 'It is mine to avenge; I will repay,' says the Lord.

~Romans 12:19

If you checked...

2. Wait awhile. Soon she'll be hurt be someone else, and you can gloat.

 ## Consider This

Why waste time waiting? Get on with life.

 ## God Puts It This Way

Do not gloat when your enemy falls; when he stumbles, do not let your heart rejoice or the Lord will see and disapprove and turn his wrath away from him.

~Proverbs 24:17-18

If you checked...

3. Moan, fuss, fret, whine and feel sorry for yourself.

 ## Consider This

Perhaps you should feel sorry for the girl who hurt you. Things don't look too good for her.

 ## God Puts It This Way

Do not fret because of evil men or be envious of the wicked, for the evil man has no future hope, and the lamp of the wicked will be snuffed out.

~Proverbs 24:19-20

If you checked...

4. Be nice to her in return.

Consider This

You know the **secret to revenge**...return evil with good!

By returning a hurtful turn with a kind one, you avoid getting hurt again–by your own wrong–and you avoid hurting another person. Plus, you please God!

God Puts It This Way

Do not take revenge, my friends...On the contrary: do not be overcome by evil, but overcome evil with good.

~Romans 12:19-21

Talk to God

Dear God, (name) just hurt me. Here is what happened (tell God the situation). Lord, I want to hurt this person back. But You tell me that it is Your job to take care of this person. Today I give You this hurt. Put me in a situation with this person where I can return the wrong she did to me with good. In Jesus' name, Amen.

♪ A Note to Myself

Today's date: _____

Mark this page in a special way. Re-read it in a few days. Take note of how God is helping you return evil for good to the friend who hurt you.

The I'm Sorry Trail

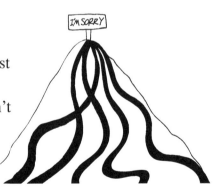

Saying "I'm sorry" is one of the hardest things any friend has to do. It's like climbing a massive mountain: you don't know how to get around it, over it or under it. The secret to saying "I'm sorry" is to pick the right trail.

Which one is the I'm Sorry Trail? Put a check next to the box.

☐ **Trail 1** You say, "I'm sorry. But even so, it's really not my fault. You made me do it."

☐ **Trail 2** You say, "I'm sorry." And then you say it again the next day, and the next day, and the next day. You don't mean to keep making the same mistake, yet you haven't changed a thing.

❑ Trail 3 You have someone else apologize for you. It's so much less embarrassing!

❑ Trail 4 Why bring up the hurt with your friend? Instead, you conveniently forget to say, "I'm sorry" so the problem can fade away quietly.

❑ Trail 5 You admit to yourself that you made the mistake, take responsibility for it, apologize to your friend, and resolve not to do it again.

✔ Check your answer!

If you checked Trail 1: You're on the Shift-the-Blame Trail. Both you and your friend may have made mistakes. But on the Shift-the-Blame Trail, you shift the entire weight of the load onto your friend's back, instead of shouldering your part. That makes your friendship harder to manage–for both of you.

If you checked Trail 2: You're on the Insincerity Trail. You say, "I'm sorry." And then you say it again the next day, and the next day and the next day. You don't mean to keep making the same mistake, yet you haven't yet changed a thing. You may actually feel regret for what you did. But an apology is insincere when you repeat the same behavior that hurt your friend in the first place. The wound keeps getting deeper each time you claim that you are sorry.

If you checked Trail 3: You're on the Pass-the-Buck Trail. Oops! You forgot one little item when you started on the Pass-the-Buck Trail: your apology. You let a messenger carry it for you instead. This trail leads nowhere. You can only get to the top of the mountain when you deliver the apology to your friend yourself.

If you checked Trail 4: You're on the Avoid Confrontation Trail. Try as you might, you can't stay on the Avoid Confrontation Trail for long until you reach a fork in the road. One fork leads to major roadblocks. Your friendship can't go on. The hurt hasn't had the chance to heal. The other fork forces you to face your friend and your problem–the very things you were trying to avoid in the first place!

If you checked Trail 5: You're on the I'm Sorry Trail! You're a hero! You're doing something that's very hard to do. You've earned the respect of others and yourself because you...

✳ Admit your mistake.

✳ Take responsibility for your mistake.

✳ Apologize to your friend.

✳ Resolve not to make the same mistake again.

 # God Puts It This Way

He who conceals his sins does not prosper, but whoever confesses and renounces them finds mercy.

~Proverbs 28:13

 # What God Means

Want a happy friendship? Admit your mistakes!

 # Talk to God

Dear God, I want to take the I'm Sorry Trail. I think I hurt my friend. It's hard for me to admit my mistake (name a mistake you made with your friend). Give me the strength to go to her, tell her I'm sorry, ask her to forgive me and not do it again. I trust You to help me do this. In Jesus' name, Amen.

● Make It! ● Friendship Forgiveness Board

Use this fun board to write down day-to-day reminders. As you wipe it clean each time, remember how you can also wipe your heart clean when you forgive someone.

 ## What You Need

* ✳ foam board or poster board
* ✳ solid or lightly-patterned adhesive-backed plastic
* ✳ ruler
* ✳ scissors
* ✳ emery board (optional)
* ✳ spring-type clothespin
* ✳ wipe-off marker
* ✳ craft foam
* ✳ hot glue gun
* ✳ craft glue
* ✳ heavy duty double-sided tape or mounting squares

What to Do

1. Measure and cut the foam board or poster board to the size you want your board to be.

2. If desired, smooth the rough edges of the foam board with an emery board.

3. Measure and cut adhesive-backed plastic to cover one side of the board, allowing 1½ inches extra on each side to turn to the back.

4. Apply adhesive-backed plastic to the board and turn the edges to the back, smoothing out any air bubbles as you go.

5. Clip the wipe-off marker onto the clothespin. Place the clothespin on the board in the spot you choose. Adjust as needed. Lightly mark the clothespin location with a pencil.

6. Ask an adult to help you hot glue the clothespin into place.

7. Cut out craft foam decorations. Place them on the board and clothespin. Adjust as needed. Use craft glue to secure them in place.

8. Attach double-sided tape or mounting squares on the back of the board. Or, tape a string on the back for hanging.

9. When the board is dry, hang it in a convenient spot.

10. Write reminders on your new **Friendship Board**...and wipe them clean with **Forgiveness!**

Hint: Test your wipe-off marker on an extra piece of adhesive-backed plastic before you use it on your board.

Chapter Ten

Be Friends with You

"Seek peace and pursue it."

~Psalm 34:14

✳ How Can You Be Friends with You? ✳

Use Your Time Well.

You spend a lot of time with yourself (yeah, like 24/7!). You always will. Make the most of it!

Like Yourself.

It's okay to think you are okay! (You only become conceited, arrogant or snobby when you think you are better than other people instead of just different from them.)

Know Yourself.

You have strengths and weaknesses. Learn what they are.

Be Realistic.

Expect that you'll make mistakes, hurt yourself and have to forgive yourself.

Stay Balanced.

Keep a balance between time alone and time with people.

You Are Never Alone!

Make it a twosome. Always include God!

QUIZ! Timeout from People

Have you ever felt like any of these girls? Circle Yes or No, then add them up to see what your answers reveal about you.

Natasha is mad at Kendall because Kendall spent Friday night at Lana's house. Lana wants to know why Meg didn't come with Kendall. Meg tried to explain that she had already promised Lucy that she'd call her that evening, and when she did, her mom told her they had family plans. You are frustrated and exhausted trying to keep up with it all.

Yes   No

You have a Spanish test tomorrow and you HAVE to study. The moose calls plunging through your bedroom walls are actually your brother, who is practicing his tuba. Moose Boy is too loud even for Dad, who turns up the TV so he can hear the baseball game. When the oven timer buzzes and Mom yells, "Could someone please take the casserole out?" you feel an irresistible urge to crawl under your bed and hibernate until you're 20.

Yes   No

Oh, no. Audrey is waiting for you at your locker…again. Her parents must have had another argument. You've been a good friend and listened to Audrey through it all. But you wish she didn't share every detail of every argument her parents have had for the last three months. Ugh!

Yes   No

A flashback of your evening: tidy up your room, answer the phone and take a message for your mom, eat dinner, call your friend Layla, do your math homework, call Layla back, pack your backpack for tomorrow, talk with Devin when she calls you, ask your mom to sign your field trip permission slip, chat with Grandma when she calls to check on you, put away your laundry, make arrangements to carpool with Jeff to the youth group meeting…suddenly, when the phone rings again you feel you can't talk to one other person or your lips will fall off.

Yes   No

 Check your answers

If you answered mostly Yes
You need a Timeout From People! Too much to do, too much noise, too much confusion, too much information and too many needs all add up to one thing: take a break. Spend time with you. Alone. P.S. Include **The Friendship Coach** in your "alone time."

If you answered mostly No
Be prepared! Sooner or later, you'll need some time away from others. Don't wait until your Time With People goes into overload. Get some "alone time" before you feel you'll pass out without it.

 God Puts It This Way
Seek peace and pursue it.
~Psalm 34:14

 **Talk to God**

Dear God, I know sometimes I need time alone with You. Give me the wisdom to know when to take a break from people. In Jesus' name, Amen.

 **Alone and Okay**

Am I Weird?

Q: I play the violin. Lessons and rehearsals take up a lot of my time and I enjoy practicing. But my friends at school don't get it. They say it's too much work and keeps me too busy. But my friend Judy from the youth orchestra says she feels the same way I do about her cello. Is it okay that I like practicing when almost everyone I know thinks it's weird?

A: Hooray for you! You're okay spending time alone with your violin. You are already a winner in **The Friendship Game** because:

✳ You have found an activity that you love.

✳ You're willing to spend some time alone, working at the violin.

✳ You have found a friend–Judy–who understands how you feel about music.

Not Bored

Q: My friend Carrie doesn't understand how to have fun alone. When she doesn't have a friend over, she's on the phone or on-line IM-ing. I like being alone so I can write in my journal, read a good book or play on the computer by myself. Does this make me too much of a loner?

A: Hooray for you! You are a winner in **The Friendship Game** because:

❋ You can entertain yourself. This makes you a more interesting person.

❋ You're not afraid to get to know you! And there's nothing lonely about that.

Keep Going!

Q: I'm working hard to be good at friendship, both with others and by myself. But lots of times, I feel like I'm the only one who's trying to go about it in the right way. I know God is on my side, but I still feel lonely and alone. Help!

A: Hooray for you! You are already a winner in **The Friendship Game**, even if you don't feel like it. Here's why:

❋ You recognize that being a good friend takes some effort.

❋ You think for yourself, rather than going along with the crowd's ideas about friendship ("peer pressure").

👉 Try This

Ask **The Friendship Coach** to help you find one or two friends who can relate to your good efforts. That way, you can encourage each other and you won't feel so alone in **The Friendship Game**.

God Puts It This Way

Encourage one another and build each other up.

~1 Thessalonians 5:11

Talk to God

Dear God, You know what I need: encouragement. Please send me a friend who is trying to be a winner in **The Friendship Game**. If this person is in my life already, show me who she is. I want to encourage her, too. Thank You, Coach! In Jesus' name, Amen.

♪ A Note to Myself

Today's date: _____

Write the date above when God sends a special friend into your life who shares your goal of being a winner in **The Friendship Game**!

10 Fun Things to Do with You

1. Experiment with your hair–try a different style!

2. Sort through your closet. Match up tops and bottoms that you've never tried together before.

3. Record a list of all the things you'd like to do in your life.

4. Use a mirror to draw a self-portrait.

5. Write a letter to yourself. Sign and date it. Open it one year (or one month, or one week) from today.

6. Memorize a Bible verse that's special to you. Write each word on a separate index card. Mix up the cards. Put them back in the right order.

7. Write a letter or an e-mail to an MK (Missionary Kid).

8. Make up new words to a favorite song.

9. Try on all the jewelry in your jewelry box.

10. Make a **Just-4-Me Journal**. Turn to page 155 to find out how!

Things You Like About You

"Once Upon a Time" is not just a fairy tale! Complete each of the following sentences by telling a true story of what happened to you.

One time, I told a joke that made a hard situation better. Here's what happened:

_____

_____

_____

One time, I gave a friend a compliment. I felt really good later. Here's what happened:

_____

_____

_____

One time, I worked really hard at something and I'm glad I did. Here's what happened:

_____

_____

_____

One time, I showed another person how to do something. It seemed insignificant at the time, but I still felt happy about it. Here's what happened:

_____

_____

_____

One time, I visited a sick friend. Here's what happened:

_____

_____

_____

_____

One time, I obeyed my parents without being reminded. Here's what happened:

_____

_____

_____

Real Girl TIPS

"When I'm alone, I talk to God. It's just me and Him."

Becca, age 10
California

_____

Real Girl TIPS

"I like being by myself because it gives me time to just think."

Jenna, age 12
Indiana

One time, I invited a friend to a program at church. Here's what happened:

_____

_____

_____

_____

One time, I noticed that a friend needed help and I was able to help her. Here's what happened:

_____

_____

_____

Now learn what your real-life stories reveal about you!

You might think it's not nice to think highly of yourself. So maybe you find it hard to make a list of things you like about you. But here is why it's right to like you for you:

✳ You have special gifts and abilities not because of anything you have done, but because God gave them to you.

God Puts It This Way

Every good and perfect gift is from above, coming down from the Father of the heavenly lights, who does not change like shifting shadows.

~James 1:17

✳ Things you like about you are neither to be hidden away...nor bragged about. God gives you those special gifts to use for Him.

God Puts It This Way

Let your light shine before men, that they may see your good deeds and praise your Father in heaven.

~Matthew 5:16

✳ It's okay to enjoy your special gifts and abilities as long as you give God thanks for them and use them properly.

God Puts It This Way

For everything God created is good, and nothing is to be rejected if it is received with thanksgiving.

~1 Timothy 4:4

Talk to God

Dear God, I feel awkward telling You that I like some things about myself (name some of them). But I see that the best way to thank You for these gifts is to use them well. Help me to always do that. Remind me if I do not. I want to please You! In Jesus' name, Amen.

● Make It! ● Just-4-Me Journal

A journal is a place to write your secret thoughts. Use it to record what you're learning about friendship, to draw pictures or to just doodle! **Just-4-Me Journal** is your special book.

What You Need

❋ notebook with cardboard cover (not spiral-bound)

❋ polar fleece

❋ decorative trim (optional)

❋ craft glue

❋ fabric glue

❋ scissors

❋ ruler

What to Do

1. Spread out the polar fleece on a flat surface. Lay open the notebook on top of the fleece. Cut the fleece around the notebook, allowing 1 to 2 inches of extra fleece on each side.

2. Leave the front cover of the notebook on top of the fleece. Close the back cover of the notebook onto the front. Spread craft glue on the cardboard back of the notebook, making sure the glue reaches all the way to the edges and along the spine. Fold the right side of the fleece over the back cover. Smooth out the fabric.

3. Repeat the process for the front cover this way: Turn the notebook over onto its glued back cover. Lay open the left side of the fabric. With the front cover of the notebook closed, spread craft glue on the entire cardboard front, making sure the glue reaches all the way to the edges and along the spine. Fold the left side of the

fleece over the front cover. Smooth out the fabric. Allow the glue to dry completely.

4. Trim away excess fabric along the cardboard cover edges.

5. To add a pocket for pens and pencils, first cut a piece of polar fleece measuring 3" x 5½". Position the pocket on the front of your journal. Use fabric glue to attach the pocket to the journal, leaving the top of the pocket open. Attach decorative trim around the edges of the pocket with fabric glue.

6. To add a matching placeholder, first figure out the placeholder length: measure the height of the notebook and add 6 inches to that number. Cut a piece of polar fleece measuring ½-inch wide by the placeholder length. With craft glue, attach one end of the placeholder to the upper left inside back cover of the journal. Fringe the free end of the placeholder. Allow the glue to dry completely. Open to the page you wish to mark in your journal and position the placeholder from back to front, laying it in that page.

Real Girl TIPS

"The best part about being alone is getting to choose what I want to do."

Lauren, age 12
Maryland

7. Write a special entry in your **Just-4-Me Journal!**

Chapter Eleven

F.O.O.K.s
(Friends of Other Kinds)

"We have different gifts, according
to the grace given us."

~Romans 12:6

✳ A World Full of Friends! ✳

At this stage in your life, you are learning how to have and be friends with other girls your age. Each friend is a like a gift who:

✳ comes in her own unique package.

✳ can fulfill a specific need.

✳ can be a surprise!

But in addition to girls your age, you can enjoy different kinds of friends, or **F.O.O.K.s: Friends Of Other Kinds**. God will put many different people in your life. Your gift of friendship to others can be one size fits all! Read on to learn more about these F.O.O.K.s:

F.O.G.s	**Friends who are Older Girls**
F.W.G.s	**Friends Who are Guys**
F.A.F.s	**Far-Away Friends**
F.I.J.s	**Friends In Jesus**

 ## God Puts It This Way
We have different gifts, according to the grace given us.

~Romans 12:6

 ## What God Means Is
God gives us the ability to be friends with many different kinds of people.

F.O.G.s (Friends who are Older Girls)

You might have friends who may be two or three years older than you—or more. They're not quite adults, but they're not at the same age and place in life as you, either.

You've hit the **JACKPOT!**

Here's why:

❋ F.O.G.s are **clued in**.

Jackpot for you: she gets it—she knows how things work with girls your age because she was your age not long ago. She knows what you're up against, how hard it can be and how much fun it can be!

❋ F.O.G.s can give **advice**.

Jackpot for you: she's climbed through the same tangled web of the preteen years and can point out which pitfalls to avoid. She knows the special challenges and questions you are having at your age. Ask her for input!

❋ F.O.G.s can **inspire** you.

Jackpot for you: she's a living, breathing example that a girl can survive the first part of growing up. She's here to tell you about it—and to listen to you. When things feel hopeless, she can show you how what you face now will help you when you're her age.

❋ F.O.G.s can make you **feel good**.

Jackpot for you: she's cool, she's with-it—and she wants to be your friend. Enjoy it, and remember when you're her age to make friends with a preteen girl so you can pass along a great F.O.G. friendship!

Avoid F.O.G. Roadblocks!

A roadblock is an obstacle that gets in your way. Even though F.O.G. friendships can be really positive, they're also jam-packed with potential roadblocks. You can prevent collisions if you know where the roadblocks are–and how to swerve around them!

 F.O.G.s are older. She may think of you as a little kid.

 Be careful! In frustration, you might feel you have to act older than you are. Try to remember that it is your time to be your age now. Find value in that and don't rush growing up!

 F.O.G.s sometimes make mistakes. Just because she is a voice of experience doesn't mean she's always correct.

 Be careful! She's not perfect. You may be tempted to "worship" her. Remember God is the only one who is perfect and worthy of worship!

 F.O.G.s sometimes manipulate younger kids in order to feel mature.

 Be careful! In an eagerness to be accepted by her, you may be convinced to go along with anything she says, does or wants you to do–even when you know it's wrong. Don't allow any friend, even a F.O.G., to talk you into doing anything that is against your family's rules or God's rules.

F.O.G.s are making some of life's big decisions.

Be careful! She may be older, but she faces her own set of problems, and sometimes feels pressured and confused along the way. Watch and learn from her good choices, as well as her poor ones. It's easy to let your expectations be too high and think she knows it all. Don't!

God Puts It This Way

As Peter entered the house, Cornelius met him and fell at his feet in reverence. But Peter made him get up. "Stand up," he said, "I am only a man myself."

~Acts 10:25-26

Talk to God

Dear God, thank You for my F.O.G. (name your friend). It's a privilege to have an older girl as a friend. Help me to learn from her good choices and her bad choices. Give her wisdom while she becomes an adult. In Jesus' name, Amen.

FAQs: F.W.G.s (Friends Who are Guys)

It Feels Strange

Q: Christopher lives in my neighborhood, plus he's in two of my classes at school. We shoot basketball together and we have a blast. I call him to find out the homework assignments when I've been absent. I can count on him. But is it strange for me to have a guy as a good friend?

A: Right now, you may be used to thinking: friend = girl. It's easier to identify with girls, because they are most like you physically. And it's easier for you to know what girls are thinking because girls share their feelings more easily than guys. So you might think only girls can truly be friends with girls because guys are so different and you can't understand them (and they don't always get you either!). But a friend is not necessarily someone exactly like you. A friend is someone who likes you for you. If Christopher likes you and you like him, you have a friend!

A Different Way of Looking at Things

Q: I've known Zachary my whole life. He's almost like a brother to me. I talk with him about a lot of stuff that I'd never talk to my girlfriends about, like how football players tie on their shoulder pads and the best way to scale a fish. Once in awhile, Zachary turns the tables and asks me funny questions, like what it feels like to put on mascara and if skirts are uncomfortable. Is this an okay friendship?

A: You've hit on one of the best advantages to having F.W.G.s: you discover that they are not green-spotted aliens from outer space. Instead, guys are regular people who look at the world through a different set of glasses than you do. When you have an F.W.G. friendship, you get to look through their glasses along with them. (And they get to look through your glasses, too.)

It's Crush Time

Q: My friend Charity asked me at lunch yesterday if I like this guy Bryant. She said she knows I'm friends with him but she was wondering if I think he's cute. My peanut-butter sandwich started doing back flips in my stomach! I guess I'd never thought of Bryant that way. Do I have to?

A: It's crush time around you! Your friends (and maybe you, too) may be looking at guys in a different way than when you were younger. It can be confusing. But you don't have to be unprepared. There are some things you can know ahead of time:

※ Girls talk about "who likes whom"–a lot.

※ You might not be interested in guys that way yet. That's fine!

※ Your friend may have a crush on one of your F.W.G.s. That can feel very weird, especially if you're used to seeing him drag himself to the carpool at 7:30 a.m. with wet hair and a wrinkled shirt.

※ Your friends may think all girl-guy friendships are completely and totally different forever, now that you are growing up. Don't buy it. You don't need to have a crush on any and every guy that walks the face of the planet just because your friends are guy crazy! Keep being friends with F.W.G.s.

> **Real Girl TIPS**
>
> "I've known my friend Bobby all my life. He talks to me about girls he likes and I talk to him about guys I like. It's fun to get his opinion on other guys!"
>
> **Elizabeth,** age 12
> **West Virginia**

The Girl-Guy Roller-coaster

Q: Luis is one of my best buds. But lately I'm starting to look at him a little differently. What should I do? (P.S. It's scary. I don't want to mess up our friendship.)

A: You have a friend. He's a guy. You are not. It should be okay, right? But like you said, feelings between guys and girls can get more complicated as you get older. Pretty soon, you'll be thinking about romance. It's time to buckle your seatbelt! You've just climbed aboard the Girl-Guy Roller-coaster. This ride has lots of ups and downs–you'll feel on top of the world one day, and in the pits the next. But know this: the confusion you're feeling is normal. Here's how to ride and keep your F.W.G.s intact:

* All friendships go through changes! Friendships are made between people–and people don't stay the same, they grow! Expect changes. That way, you won't completely and totally freak when things feel differently.

* Examine your feelings privately. The entire lunch table doesn't need to know that you think Luis is looking good. Write in your journal, talk to a F.O.G., or e-mail an F.A.F. (see page 165). Figure out what you really think before you let your lips go flapping to your friends.

* Appreciate your F.W.G.s for what they are right now. Have fun. Keep bantering with him while you are wrestling with what you're feeling.

✳ Worried about messing up a great friendship? Do your part: be a good friend to your F.W.G. Treat him with respect rather than as a newly discovered statue. Don't forget: you're not the only one growing up. He's coping with his own mixing bowl of emotions, too.

Talk to God

Dear God, I feel strange about my friend (name your F.W.G.). Help me to be a good friend to him and appreciate his friendship while we are changing. And God, please help him, too. In Jesus' name, Amen.

F.A.F.s (Far-away Friends)

A friend who does not live nearby can still make you laugh, listen to your problems and be a good friend! Here's how some girls deal with their F.A.F.s.

I have a friend who moved to California, then back to our hometown, and then back to California. Her absence made her more special to me.

Michaela, age 12
Illinois

It's easy to take a friend for granted when you see her all the time. But an F.A.F. helps you appreciate the friends you have because you know what it feels like when they're not around anymore.

Christina, my neighbor's niece, lives in New Jersey. We get together whenever she visits her aunt. Sometimes we write letters. It's easy to feel comfortable with her even when we haven't seen each other in awhile. We have a lot in common.

Abigail, age 11
Maryland

An F.A.F. can give you confidence and self-assurance. It's encouraging to know you can have things in common and feel comfortable with a person who lives somewhere else–and that she identifies with you, too.

> I keep in touch with a friend I met at camp in Michigan. I love talking with her online. We start our conversation not knowing what is going on in each other's lives. Then we get to fill each other in. She's very special to me.
>
> Janelle, age 13
> Nebraska

You can tell an F.A.F. some things you can't or won't tell anyone nearby–without the fear that the secret will be let out of the bag. An F.A.F. can celebrate your achievements long-distance without being jealous because she's not competing with you day-to-day.

> I have a friendship with Connie and it is awesome. She lives in Greece. Even though it takes two months to get her letters, they are always interesting and funny.
>
> Mary Grace, age 13
> Maryland

An F.A.F. turns our big world into a smaller, friendlier place. It's fun to see other places and people through your friend's eyes!

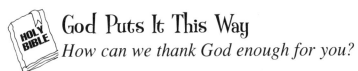

God Puts It This Way

How can we thank God enough for you?

~ 1 Thessalonians 3:9

Talk to God

Dear God, thank You for sending me a special friend. Even though I do not get to see her every day, I know we can still have a great friendship. Help me to be a good friend to her. Amen.

Spotlight on...

F.I.J.s (Friends in Jesus)

God's girls have a special group of friends who share a commitment to Jesus Christ: Friends In Jesus, or F.I.J.s.

Also Known As: believers, family of God, fellow Christians, brothers and sisters in Christ.

First established: at the beginning of time.

Qualifications: Membership as an F.I.J. is open to any person, of any age, living in any place, during any time period in history. Single qualification is faith in Jesus Christ as Lord and Savior. Membership is automatic from that moment on.

Membership totals: Huge! You can find an F.I.J. anywhere in the world, especially if you ask **The Friendship Coach** to lead you to a group of believers.

Special characteristics of F.I.J. friendships: love, acceptance, support, forgiveness, hope.

Major misunderstanding of F.I.J.s: New F.I.J.s are surprised to learn that believers argue, fight, make mistakes and are very far from perfect.

Major benefit of F.I.J.s: The totally amazing encouragement and motivation you can get from other Christians.

Strength and duration of F.I.J. friendships: F.I.J. friendships are founded on the Rock, Jesus Christ. They can endure the tests of life and last forever.

What's Unique About an F.I.J.?

✳ F.I.J.s use **The Friendship Coach's** playbook, the **Bible**, for the friendship rules and standards.

✳ F.I.J.s meet in groups at worship services, prayer meetings and Bible studies to **grow together**.

✳ F.I.J.s rely heavily on the **Holy Spirit** and **prayer** to help them get along with each other.

God Puts It This Way

Let us consider how we may spur one another on toward love and good deeds. Let us not give up meeting together, as some are in the habit of doing, but let us encourage one another.

~Hebrews 10:25-26

Write About It

Make a list of your F.I.J. friendships.

_____

_____

_____

Talk to God

Dear God, thank You for these F.I.J.s (name yours). Help me grow closer to them and support them. And along the way, help me seek out other F.I.J.s and recognize the ones You put in my life. In Jesus' name, Amen.

● Make It! ● Fantastic Friend Letter Holder

Keep your letters from F.A.F.s and other friends in this **Fantastic Friend Letter Holder**. You can also use it to store your own stationery and note cards. There's even a place for markers, pens and pencils!

 ## What You Need

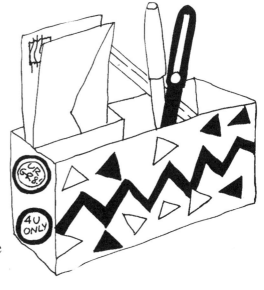

※ cereal box

※ small macaroni and cheese box (7¼-oz. size)

※ colorful paper

※ stickers (optional)

※ ruler

※ scissors

※ acid-free scrapbooking glue

※ craft glue

※ spring-type clothespins

※ pencil

What to Do

1. Stand the cereal box upright. Measure, mark and cut a line 4 inches high from the base of the box to create the letter holder.

2. Stand the macaroni and cheese box upright. Measure, mark and cut a line 4 inches high from the base of the box to create the smaller insert.

3. Cover the exterior sides of the letter holder with colorful paper by tracing the outline of each side, cutting the paper to fit and attaching the paper with acid-free scrapbooking glue.

4. Cover the two adjacent sides of the smaller insert with colorful

paper by tracing the outline of each side, cutting the paper to fit and attaching the paper with acid-free scrapbooking glue.

5. Spread craft glue on the two remaining sides and the bottom of the smaller insert. Attach the insert to one interior corner of the letter holder. Hold it in place with clothespins until dry.

6. Decorate the exterior sides of the letter holder by cutting colorful paper strips, squares, triangles and other designs, and attaching them with acid-free scrapbooking glue. You can also add stickers, if you like.

7. Organize your letter-writing supplies in your new **Fantastic Friend Letter Holder**, and write a letter to an F.A.F.!

Hint: Use acid-free scrapbooking glue to prevent paper from wrinkling when it is glued to other paper or cardboard.

Chapter Twelve

Your A.B.F.F.

(Absolute Best Friend Forever)

"Surely I am with you always, to the very end of the age."

~Matthew 28:20

✳ Why Jesus Is Your A.B.F.F. ✳

Have you ever wished for...

☐ A **friend** who will be your friend no matter what?

☐ A **friend** who will be closer to you than anyone?

☐ A **friend** who will be your friend forever?

If you checked any boxes above, here is a surprise: You can have Jesus as your A.B.F.F. (Absolute Best Friend Forever)!

3 Reasons Why Jesus Is Your A.B.F.F.

1 Jesus is your **absolute** friend.

Absolute = unchanging, firm, like a rock, steady, constant, invariable, unfailing, reliable

Jesus is your **absolute** friend because He never changes. You can always count on Him!

God Puts It This Way

Jesus Christ is the same yesterday and today and forever.

~Hebrews 13:8

Jesus is your **best** friend.

Best = ultimate, ideal, number one, greatest, total, extreme, numero uno, the max, perfect

Jesus is your **best** friend because He is better at it than anyone ever is, ever has been or ever will be. He's perfect!

 God Puts It This Way
The Son…has been made perfect forever.
~Hebrews 7:28

 Jesus is your best friend **forever**.

Forever = always, for eternity, 'til the end of time, infinity

Jesus is your best friend **forever** because He is alive **forever**, promises you'll be alive **forever** if you believe in Him and promises to be with you **forever**!

 God Puts It This Way
Surely I am with you always, to the very end of the age.
~Matthew 28:20

 Talk to God

Dear God, wow, I never thought about it like this before: Jesus can be my absolute friend, my best friend and my friend forever. I want that. Jesus, please be my friend. Show me how to rely on You. And help me be a good friend to You, too. In Your precious name, Amen.

 **But My Idea of Jesus Was...**

What Does He Look Like?

Q: It's hard for me to think of Jesus as my friend. I picture Him as a guy with a beard and a robe walking around with a lamb in His arms, patting little kids on the head. Is that what He's really like?

A: SHORT ANSWER

Maybe. No one is still alive from Bible times to give us a definite "Yep, that's Him!" or "No way!" And the Bible contains very little physical description of Jesus.

LONG ANSWER

1. Jesus lived on the earth 2000 years ago. Electric razors weren't invented yet, so most men wore beards.

2. In Palestine where Jesus lived, men wore long robes.

3. Back then, sheep and lambs were everywhere, like dogs and cats are today. They were not pets, however. Shepherding was a business.

4. Jesus loves kids. It is very likely that He patted them on the head, hugged them and invited them to sit on His lap.

5. You may have gotten your idea of Jesus from a painting or book in Sunday school. While it may be true, it is incomplete. There's a lot more to Jesus!

Do's and Don'ts

Q: My idea of Jesus is that He has a list of do's and don'ts. When I follow the do's, He leaves me alone. When I slip up with a few don'ts, He gets mad at me. It's hard to think of Him as my friend if He's really like that. Is He?

A: ### SHORT ANSWER

No, He's not like that.

LONG ANSWER

1. Jesus never leaves you alone, even when you don't feel He is near.

2. Jesus wants you to know the difference between right and wrong (do's and don'ts), so you can choose to do things His way.

3. Jesus knows you will mess up (because you are human), but He loves you anyway.

4. Rather than being angry when you confess your mistakes, Jesus loves to forgive!

God Puts It This Way

There will be more rejoicing in heaven over one sinner who repents than over ninety-nine righteous persons who do not need to repent.

~Luke 15:7

What's His Real Name?

Q: Who are people talking about when they say, "Jesus is your friend"? Some people say that His name is "God." Some call Him "Jesus." Some call Him "Lord." My idea is that Jesus and God are two completely different people. Am I right?

A: ### Short Answer

Not really.

Long Answer

1. Do you call your father "Dad"? Other people may call him "Joe" or "Mr. Smith." Your grandparents call him "Son." But all of those names still belong to the same person.

2. "God," "Jesus," "Lord" and other names given to God represent different facets of God's personality. But they all belong to the same Person.

3. "Jesus" is a special part of God's personality. He is called "God's Son." Jesus came down from heaven and showed us how to live on earth. He was fully human and fully God. So He understands us completely–and can truly be our Absolute Friend.

God Puts It This Way

[Jesus said], "I no longer call you servants...Instead, I have called you friends."

~John 15:15

Church

Q: I thought you could only be friends with Jesus if you go to church. Is that true?

A: **SHORT ANSWER**

No.

LONG ANSWER

1. Jesus was friendly with many different kinds of people in Bible times, whether or not they belonged to a church.

2. Churches are made up of people who share a common bond. They want to worship Jesus, serve Him and tell other people about Him. But church is not an exclusive club.

3. Jesus wants believers to attend church so that they can encourage each other.

4. You can be friends with Jesus whenever, wherever and whoever you are.

How Can I Have Jesus as My Friend?

Q: I want Jesus to be my friend. How do I do that?

A: **SHORT ANSWER**

Ask Him!

LONG ANSWER

1. Tell God that you know you make mistakes and you are sorry.

2. Tell God that you know you need Him to help you.

3. Ask Him to forgive you.

4. Invite Jesus to be your Friend and Lord of your life.

5. Trust Him with your life.

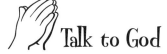 Talk to God

Dear God, I know I have made mistakes (name any mistakes that come to mind). Please forgive me. Lord Jesus, please come into my heart and show me how to live. I want You to be my Friend for life. In Jesus' name, Amen.

 A Note to Myself

Today's date: _____ Today, I asked Jesus to be my friend!*

> *If you prayed this prayer for the first time today, make sure you tell an F.I.J. so she can celebrate with you!

8 Ways to Dress for Friendship Success

It seems so simple: Love Jesus by loving others. But sometimes it's not easy.

❊ You might feel that you've made a mistake or believe in someone who is not real–especially when Jesus seems far away.

❊ You might feel as though you're all alone–especially when you're around others who don't know Jesus as a friend.

❊ You might feel badly when you deliberately ignore Jesus and "do your own thing–especially when you remember how Jesus has forgiven you.

The Friendship Coach knows that keeping close to Jesus can be hard–and being a friend to others at the same time can be even harder. He has worked out a special way for God's girls to handle this problem. You may be surprised to learn that there are 8 ways to dress for friendship success.

1. Be ready. Have the proper clothes in order.

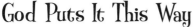

God Puts It This Way

Therefore put on the full armor of God, so that when the day of evil comes, you may be able to stand your ground, and after you have done everything, to stand.

~Ephesians 6:13

2. Listen to and speak the truth. You'll need a belt.

God Puts It This Way

Stand firm then, with the belt of truth buckled around your waist.

~Ephesians 6:14

3. Do the right thing, even when it's hard. Always wear a clean shirt.

God Puts It This Way

Stand firm, then... with the breastplate of righteousness in place.

~Ephesians 6:14

4. Live peaceably. Get along with others. Tie your shoes to prevent tripping.

God Puts It This Way

[Have] your feet fitted with the readiness that comes from the gospel of peace.

~Ephesians 6:15

5. Expect hard times. Put on a coat to guard against storms.

 ## God Puts It This Way
Take up the shield of faith, with which you can extinguish all the flaming arrows of the evil one.

~Ephesians 6:16

6. Remember what Jesus did for you. Protect your head–and your faith–with a hat.

 ## God Puts It This Way
Take the helmet of salvation.

~Ephesians 6:17

7. Use the Coach's playbook. Read the Bible along the way.

 ## God Puts It This Way
Take...the sword of the Spirit, which is the word of God.

~Ephesians 6:17

8. Pray. Keep talking with **The Friendship Coach!**

 ## God Puts It This Way
Pray in the Spirit on all occasions with all kinds of prayers and requests.

~Ephesians 6:18

 ## Talk to God

Dear God, remind me when I forget to put on an article of Friendship Clothing. Show me how to wear them all properly. In Jesus' name, Amen.

Jesus' Friendship Formula

Jesus did something for you that no other friend can do…And He wants you to share it with your friends, too! Jesus uses a special formula to describe the two parts of your friendship with Him.

Jesus' Friendship Formula

What Jesus Did

"Greater love has no one than this, that he lay down his life for his friends." (John 15:13)

What He Wants You to Do

"You are my friends if you do what I command…love each other." (John 15:14, 17)

What Jesus Did

Friendship with Jesus is based on His amazing love. He laid down His life for you!

✳ Jesus knows that no matter how hard you try, you can't be perfect.

✳ Jesus knows that you can't be close to God unless someone pays for your mistakes.

✳ Jesus knew that only He could pay for your mistakes, because He's perfect.

✳ Jesus paid for your mistakes by laying down His life…and dying on the cross.

What a friend!!!

What He Wants You to Do

Jesus asks you to do something different from what He did.

✳ Accept what He did for you and be His friend.

✳ Show Him that you love Him by loving others.

☞ Think About This

Jesus does His part. Do yours!

Talk to God

Dear God, You are so awesome! Thank You for sending Jesus to be my friend. Jesus, thank You for laying down Your life for me. I accept Your amazing gift of friendship love. Lord, I want to do my part. Help me to love other people around me. May they see Your love shining through me. In Jesus' name, Amen.

● Make It! ● The Absolute Best Pencil Topper

The King of kings is your A.B.F.F.! This pencil topper looks like a crown belonging to the King, yet you can make it from materials you already have at home. Plus, the glitter and jewels remind you that Jesus' love always shines through!

What You Need

✳ pencil

✳ 1-oz. snack bag

✳ moistened paper towel

✳ clear tape

✳ scissors

✳ ruler

✳ glitter glue

✳ paint pens

✳ small acrylic rhinestones or sequins

What to Do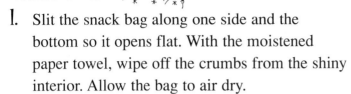

1. Slit the snack bag along one side and the bottom so it opens flat. With the moistened paper towel, wipe off the crumbs from the shiny interior. Allow the bag to air dry.

2. Measure and cut a 5½" by 5½" square from the snack bag. Lay the square on your work surface with the shiny side face down. Position the eraser-end of the pencil in the bottom right-hand corner of the square, with one inch of the pencil on the square. Tape the pencil end onto the square.

3. Roll the pencil and the snack bag square away from you. This produces a thin tube with the shiny side of the square on the outside, creating the pencil topper. When finished, tape the square corner into place on the pencil.

4. Use scissors to fringe the pencil topper ends 3 inches deep.

5. With glitter glue, cover the tape where the snack bag square touches the pencil. Add rhinestones or sequins as desired.

6. With a paint pen or glitter glue, draw a cross on the shaft of the pencil topper.

7. Use **The Absolute Best Pencil Topper** to write in your **Just-4-Me Journal** (see page 155) or as you work through the exercises in this book.

Hint: Glitter-covered or foil-covered pencils work especially well for this craft.

Answers to Did You Know?

Page 50 (top)
Paul motivated and mobilized others. He was the Christian church's first missionary. Read about his mission trips in the book of Acts.

Page 50 (bottom)
Andrew was known for recruiting others to "join the team." Read about how he introduced Simon Peter to Jesus in John 1:40-42.

Page 51
Barnabas was known for being an encourager, and was a deacon in the early Christian church. Read about him in the book of Acts.

Page 73
Queen Esther kept her Jewish bloodline a secret. She was faithful to God, and she became Queen of Persia. When the enemies of Israel attempted to wipe out the Jewish people, Esther revealed her nationality and saved the Jews from destruction. Read the whole story in the book of Esther.

Page 98
Arrows! Read about it in 1 Samuel 20.

Page 103
Neither! Jesus **was not** a Pharisee or a Sadducee. In fact, He often clashed with them and was rejected by them.

Page 110
Jesus had a close group of friends. There were 12 of them, and they were called his disciples.

Page 128
Judas betrayed Jesus for 30 pieces of silver. Read about it in Matthew 27:3-5.

More Real Girl TIPS

"When I meet a new friend at church or in school, I find a way I can team up with her. Then I can get to know her better."

Annie
age 9
Minnesota

"The worst day of my life was the first day at my new school. Only one person talked to me. I cried the whole way home. But it got better as time went on."

Tori
age 13
Maryland

"I share my room with my sister. She's noisy. I like having the room to myself because then it's quiet."

Ariel
age 13
Kansas

"When Jess started to ignore me, it really hurt. It hurt worse when she said she was saving her seat for her other 'friend.' It took time, but I made new friends that didn't treat me like Jess did."

Stacey
age 10
Maryland

"When I'm around other people, I pay attention to them. When I'm by myself, I can figure out what I think and believe without being distracted. It's easier to concentrate."

Robin
age 11
Georgia

"Read, paint, draw, write–my ideas flow when I'm working by myself!"

Tiffany
age 13
Pennsylvania

"Leanna is a year older than me. She is a special friend because she knows how it is for girls my age–plus she listens and helps."

Molly
age 11
Maryland

"Being by myself is something I need. Sometimes I just want to be alone and write in my journal."

Andria
age 12
Maryland

"Jesus is my #1 Friend!"

Charlene
age 13
Minnesota

Friend File!

My best friend is:

_____

Because:

_____

_____

Our favorite thing to do together is:

_____

_____

Another of my friends is:

_____

We like to:

_____

Someone with whom I would like to be friends is:

_____

Because:

_____

The Secret to Friendship is:

_____

I know Jesus is my friend because:

_____

L48220

THE GIRL'S GUIDE TO LIFE

Ages 10–12, 192 pages, Paperback, Illustrated.
The Girl's Guide to Life is for girls who want a road map to lead them through life's journey. *The Girl's Guide to Life* points to the Bible, the best map of all, talks about issues girls face like family, friends, boys, school, money, nutrition, fitness, and standing firm when temptations appear. Ages 10–12.

THE GIRL'S GUIDE FOR PRETEENS

L48213

Ages 10–12, 176-208 pages, Paperback.
Encourage girls with these fun and creative books covering issues that matter most to preteens: fashion, being their best, making friends, understanding the Bible, getting along with Mom, dealing with money, and LIFE! Ages 10–12.

L48211

L48212

L48213

L48214

L48215

L48216

L48217

L48218

L48219

GOD'S GIRLS Fun Crafts Plus Devotions!

Ages 9–12, 184 pages, Paperback, Illustrated.
Preteen girls will be captivated by this book, with devotions about Biblical women and crafts created especially for girls. Weaving belts, decorating rooms and party planning activities all teach girls that fun and faith are part of God's plan. Ages 9–12.

L48011

THE GOD AND ME!® BIBLE

Ages 6–9, 192 pages, Paperback, Full Color Illustrations. Designed to capture the vivid imaginations of growing girls, The God and Me! Bible puts God's Word inot the hearts and minds. The bright illustrations, creative activities, puzzles, and games that accompany each Bible story make learning important Bible truths both fun and easy. Ages 6–9.

L48522

JUST FOR ME! FOR GIRLS

Ages 6–9, 152 pages, Paperback, Illustrated.
Through Stories, crafts, and fun activities, younger girls will discover what they need to grow closer to God! Ages 6–9.

L48413

L48412

L48411

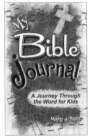

L46911   **DB46731**

GUIDED JOURNALS FOR GIRLS AND BOYS

Ages 10–12, 136–160 pages, Paperback, Illustrated. Preteen boys and girls will love these daily devotional journals that really encourage them to dig into the Bible.